A TASTE OF PUNJAB

LALI NAYAR

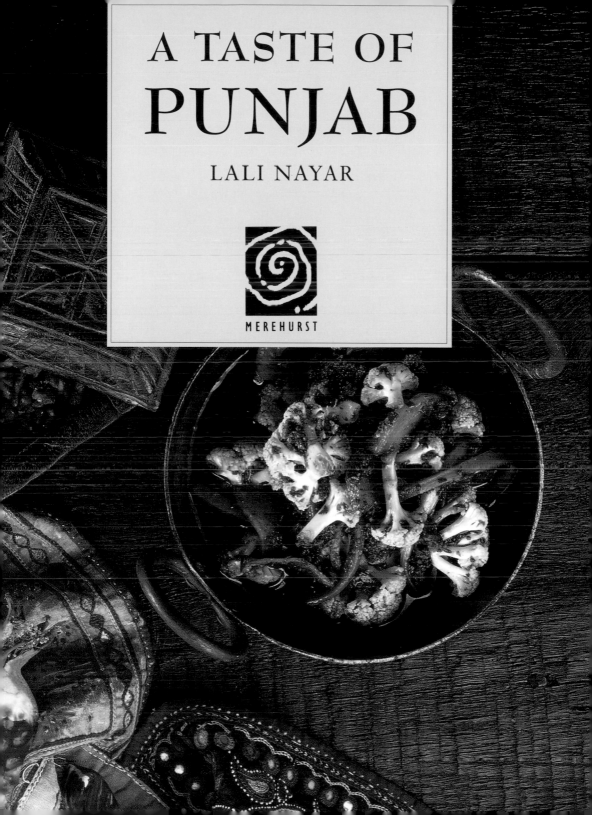

A TASTE OF
PUNJAB

LALI NAYAR

MEREHURST

Published in 1995 by Merehurst Ltd
Ferry House, 51-57 Lacy Road, Putney London SW15 1PR

Copyright © Lali Nayar
ISBN 1 85391 414 2

Edited by **Val Barrett**
Designed by **Sara Kidd**
Photography by **Steve Baxter**
Styling by **Marian Price**
Food for Photography by **Annie Nichols**

Colour separation by Global Colour, Malaysia
Printed by Craftprint, Singapore

Previous pages: Bhatura (p.93), Khabuli Chole (p.69), and Khatta Mitha Achaar (p.105).

A BIG THANK YOU :
To my dear husband, Manjit, whose encouragement
has enabled me to become an author.
To my son, Aj, who typed my messy manuscript with
patience, understanding and diligence.
To my daughter, Priti, for providing me with endless
cups of tea.

CONTENTS

INTRODUCTION

India, with its enormous geographical and human diversity is a wonderland of the East. Within its boundaries are many different states, which in turn have different physical, historical, social and cultural aspects. Deeply embedded in the many regions lie the variations of cooking as well as the eating habits of the people. I think food, more than anything else, is a great dividing factor and a major essential in labelling the differences among the far flung regions of India.

The well used words "variety is the spice of life" cannot ring more true than within the realms of regional Indian cuisine. It provides an astonishing mosaic of taste, texture, flavour and appearance which is vast, varied and bewildering. However, in spite of all this diversity, there is the underlying unity of a majority of the ingredients used and that forces the regions to shed their individuality to some extent and come under the blanket term of making "Indian food". Even so, the many superb regional culinary styles have definite characteristics.

A legendary one amongst them is Punjabi cuisine which has no doubt been responsible to a great extent for promoting the love of Indian food outside India.
Lying in the Northwest region of India, Punjab, or the land of the 5 rivers, has a cuisine which over the years has been influenced by a string of invaders such as the Persians, Afghans, Greeks and Mongols. This has resulted in the cuisine now being not only rich and exotic, but robust and earthy as well. The indomitable, spirited Punjabis have acquired a reputation for being the greatest food lovers in India, whose tantalisingly, tasty and nutritious preparations are as full of zest as the people themselves. To help them further, the soil, climate and geographical position of Punjab supply rich produce and enables Punjabis to make food that can be a gastronomic discovery, especially for those who are new to Indian cuisine.

For the many who are familiar with the regions hearty fare, the words "Taste of Punjab" can conjure up many images of which the "Tandur" would perhaps be the one most associated with Punjabi cuisine. The word "Tandur", which is now synonymous with Indian cuisine, has its home in Punjab, and from there many excellent tanduri dishes have found their way all around the globe.

I hope this introduction to the food of Punjab, by way of these typical, traditional and well-loved recipes, will give you a true insight and taste of some of the regions wonderful preparations.

While it is often said that one cannot learn enough about food, we are fortunate to live in times where the increasing mobility of people allows many of us to know and experiment with different kinds of food. I certainly hope my selection of recipes, which are based on tested practice and merit, provide a feast of joy to all those who relish good cooking and adventurous eating. For me, Punjabi cuisine is *"Food that I can eat to my heart's content"*.

Easy Route to Confident Punjabi Cooking

Hints and Tips

Punjabi food is "spicy hot" and not "chilli hot". The hotness of spices stimulates and tickles the palate, whereas the hotness of chillies can paralyse the tongue! How hot a dish becomes is a matter of personal taste as you can always increase or decrease the use of red chillies, which are the real culprits!

As far as possible, do grind your spices freshly as this will make an enormous difference in producing a more flavoursome dish. Dry, whole spices remain fresh for long periods if they are stored in air-tight jars and kept in a dry, cool and dark place.

To help in making a dish correctly, remember to follow the recipe closely. Use the given proportions and quantities of ingredients and keep to the sequence of cooking them. It is a good idea to collect all the ingredients and equipment before beginning to cook.

Many large supermarkets now sell commercial brands of ready-made pastes and powders of various blends to serve as shortcuts in many Indian dishes. I find them useful only if I am pressed for time, but given a choice I would rather make my own, to give a genuine fresh taste that a good recipe deserves! Prepackaged garammasalas and other powdered spices can restrict the flavours, and dishes can lose some of their distinct aromas.

I find the ready prepared, bottled forms of chopped garlic, grated ginger and ground chillies very handy to have in the store cupboard for those occasions when time is short. Another very useful product to keep, is a packet of deep fried onions.

Cooking Utensils

The pots and pans in any average kitchen will suffice to make the recipes in this book, but given below is a list of traditional equipment that is found in most Punjabi homes. It would be useful to have these or something similar to help in the preparations.

Chakla Velana: Chakla is a small marble or wooden platform. Velana is a wooden rolling pin used for rolling Indian breads like chapatis, parathas etc.

Chimta: These are tongs which are especially handy when cooking Indian breads.

Doari Danda: A two-piece grinding stone used to grind fresh masalas and other pastes. A pestle and mortar can be used instead.

Deg: A large pot, traditionally made of brass or copper, but these days, stainless steel has come into vogue.

Kadhai: A deep and circular, wok-like frying pan with handles. It is usually made of cast iron or stainless steel and should ideally have a heavy base.

Kadhchi: A long-handled ladle used for stirring.

Kaddukas: A hand grater.

Kulfi-de-Saanche: Cone shaped aluminium moulds about 7.5-10cm (3-4 inches) long. Used for freezing kulfi (Indian ice-cream). You can use small yogurt cartons instead.

Malmal-da-Tukda: A piece of Muslin cloth.

Masale Daani: A spice box. These traditional boxes can be bought in Indian grocery stores.

Parat: A utensil in which dough is kneaded. It is a wide shallow dish, often made of stainless steel.

Patila: A pot which has straight sides and a horizontal rim.

Pauni: A slotted frying spoon.

Seekha: Thick skewers for barbecuing. They are about 30-38cm (12-15 inches) long and are pointed at one end and square in cross section so they are flat on all four sides. This style of skewer holds the food better than the rod shaped skewer.

Tandur: The "tandur" is a cylindrical shaped clay oven, which is traditionally heated by charcoal. It comes in various sizes, is open at both ends with the base being wider than the top. Generally placed on, or even in, the ground, it essentially calls for an outdoor style of cooking. Charcoal is spread evenly across the bottom and this enables the temperature to rise gradually and the clay sides to remain hot for long periods of time.

The origins of the "tandur" cannot be pinpointed to a single area as clay ovens of some form were, and are still, used in and around various parts of the world. But one thing is certain - that within the Punjab lies the home of the well-loved, unique and remarkable "tanduri" style of cuisine, which in a nutshell is "incomparable".

Special Fresh Ingredients
Garammasala (Mixture of Hot Spices)

India is the spice bowl of the world, and it is no wonder that spices, and the art of blending spices, really form the basis of Indian cooking. A combination of various "hot spices" that is highly aromatic is known as garammasala. It can be added to dishes towards the end of cooking or used as part of a marinade, it can also be sprinkled over a dish as a garnish, just before serving.

Garammasala has no set formula that one can follow to make, as it can be made in a variety of combinations according to one's own preferences. Some regions in India do seem to have a certain "type" of garammasala which is typical to the area. The following type of garammasala is generally associated with Punjabi cuisine.

To make 60g (2 oz) garammasala:
22g (³/₄ oz) brown cardamoms
22g (³/₄ oz) cinnamon stick
7g (¹/₄ oz) black cumin seeds
7g (¹/₄ oz) whole cloves
10 black peppercorns
large pinch of fresh grated nutmeg

1. Shell the cardamoms.
2. In a grinder, put the cardamom seeds, cinnamon, cumin seeds, cloves, peppercorns

and nutmeg. Run the machine until they blend into a fine powder..
3. Store immediately in an airtight container. It lasts well, but not indefinitely, and it is better to make it fresh in small amounts to get the best flavours.

Ghee (Clarified Butter)

Ghee is commonly used as a medium for cooking all over India, but in the Punjab, it is definitely a "firm favourite". The older generation of Punjabis found it unthinkable to cook in anything apart from ghee, and I can still hear my grandmother saying "if it is not made in ghee, don't eat it, it will spoil your health!" Of course, things change with time - so the attitude towards ghee has changed. It is no longer the only medium used and many refined oils do equally as well. I have chosen ghee for my recipes, because I love the delicate and wonderful buttery aroma it imparts to the dishes, and because it is so typically Punjabi!

To make ghee from butter:

1. Put 900g (2lb) unsalted butter into a heavy-based saucepan and keep on a low heat. When it has melted, increase the heat and bring to the boil. Reduce the heat immediately to very low and simmer gently for 30 to 45 minutes, until all of the milk solids settle to the base of the pan and the transparent butter or ghee floats to the top.
2. Slowly transfer the liquid ghee to a bowl, by straining it through a piece of muslin. Take care not to disturb the residue left at the bottom of the pan.
3. This liquid will solidify once it is cold and can be stored in a container with a tight-fitting lid. It will keep at room temperature for 3-4 months.

Dahi (Yogurt)

The value of "dahi" or natural yogurt has been recognised in the East since ancient times, and is an integral part of Indian cuisine. In fact, no Indian meal is really complete without it. In some form or another, it finds a place for itself - eaten on its own, turned into a raita, used as a tenderiser, added to enrich gravies etc. Its versatility and healthy properties make it an invaluable item in every Indian household. As Punjab is well-blessed with the availability of milk, it is of little surprise that the daily diet of the region usually includes plenty of yogurt. It is quite easy to make natural yogurt at home by following this simple method.

To make 600ml (1 pint) natural yogurt:

600ml (1 pint) full cream milk
1 tablespoon natural yogurt

1. Put the milk in a saucepan and bring it to the boil. Remove from the heat and pour into a container. Cool until it is just slightly warm.
2. Add the yogurt and blend it in thoroughly using a whisk.

3. Cover and leave undisturbed in a warm place for several hours.

4. In hot weather, the yogurt will set in 4-5 hours and there is no need to keep it in a warm place. In a cold climate, it is best to wrap a warm blanket around the container and leave it in a warm area of the kitchen for 8-10 hours.

5. Do not disturb the container once you have left it to set.

6. Once the yogurt sets, keep the container in a fridge to prevent it from going sour. It should keep for 3-4 days.

Paneer (Home-made Cheese)

Paneer is home-made Indian cheese and a remarkable ingredient. I do not think there is any equivalent of paneer in the Western field of cookery. To call it "cottage cheese" would be wrong, as paneer does not become sticky and leathery when heated. Moreover paneer can be converted into a block and cut into pieces and then cooked, which makes it amazingly different from other types of cheese. It is an incredible source of protein and especially good for vegetarians. Surprisingly, it is a very easy cheese to make and needs no expertise or special equipment.

To make approx. 125-180g (4-6 oz) of paneer :

600ml (1 pint) full cream milk
1 tablespoon lemon juice or $1/2$ teaspoon citric acid
125ml (4 fl oz) hot water

1. Put the milk in a saucepan and bring to the boil. Stir now and then to avoid a skin forming on the top.

2. Mix the lemon juice or citric acid with the hot water. Add gradually to the milk as soon as it begins to rise, and stir gently.

3. Remove from the heat, cover and leave for about 5 minutes. The milk will then curdle and the whey will separate.

4. Strain through a muslin cloth and squeeze out all the whey. The milk mixture left in the bag is "paneer". This can be used as it is for a variety of sweet and savoury dishes, or it can be converted into a block, cut into pieces and then used.

5. To convert the paneer into a block, leave it in the muslin bag and press it down with a heavy weight for at least 2-3 hours to make a slab. This can then be cut into cubes.

6. The pieces can be used as they are, or can be deep fried to a light golden colour and then used.

7. The paneer will keep for 2-3 days in a fridge.

Basmati Rice

The long, light, fluffy grains of cooked Basmati rice look and smell totally irresistible. Many people are put off at the thought of ending up with a soggy mess when they cook rice, but it is easy to obtain a perfect result if you follow a few basic rules every time.

Always wash the rice first, as this removes a lot of the milling starch which is what makes the rice sticky. Wash the rice in several changes of water, rubbing it gently between the fingers until the water runs clear. Then the rice should be soaked in water for about 15 minutes and drained thoroughly. The soaking allows the rice grains to absorb the cooking liquid more readily and so the rice will cook faster. Never lift the lid while the rice is cooking. When almost cooked, remove from the heat and set the pan aside and leave undisturbed. It is important to let the rice relax for 5-10 minutes, to allow the rice to finish cooking in the steam within the pan. This method will ensure that you have fluffy, tender rice every time.

To cook Basmati Rice for 4:
280g (9 oz) basmati rice,
500ml (16 fl oz) water
$1/4$ teaspoon salt, optional

1. Wash the rice in several changes of water, rubbing it gently between the fingers until the water runs clear. Drain in a sieve and put in a bowl with the water. Leave for 15 minutes.
2. Put the rice, water and salt, if used, in a saucepan and bring to the boil. Boil steadily for 2 minutes and cover the pan tightly. Reduce heat to very low and cook for 10 minutes or until the rice has absorbed all the water and the grains are just tender.
3. Remove the pan from heat and leave it undisturbed for 5-10 minutes. Remove the lid and fork through the rice before serving.

Following pages: A selection of spices and seasonings used in Punjabi cooking.

Glossary
(Punjabi equivalent in brackets)

Here you will find a list of the more unusual ingredients used in Indian cooking. They are easy to find in Indian grocery stores and the equivalent Indian name has been included to help you.

Aniseed (Saunf): Small, green, aromatic seeds of the anise plant. Used for flavouring food and drinks.

Asafoetida (Hing): A strong-flavoured resin which is used in very minute quantities because of its overpowering aroma.

Bay Leaf (Tej Patta): A herb which is mostly used whole in its dried leaf form for flavouring.

Black Whole Lentils (Mah di daal): Pre-soaking for 3-4 hours is recommended for this silky textured and flavoursome lentil.

Black Eyed Beans (Lobia): Also known as small butter beans.

Buttermilk (Lassi): A thinned yogurt drink.

Cardamom, Black (Mothi illachi): An aromatic spice which is a native of India. It has a robust flavour and is an important ingredient of garammasala.

Cardamom, Green (Choti illachi): This smaller, green variety can be used along with its skin. Has a delicate aroma which makes it ideal for flavouring desserts.

Carom Seeds (Ajwain): These tiny seeds, related to the caraway and cumin, are used for seasoning savoury items. They should be used sparingly due to their very strong thyme-like flavour.

Chillies, Green (Hari Mirch): Fresh green chillies, with a delicate yet pungent taste which can be toned down if the seeds are removed.

Chillies, Red (Lal Mirch): A fiery spice, used whole or powdered in its dried form. Use according to taste or even omit altogether if desired.

Cinnamon (Dalchini): The tender, inner bark of the cinnamon tree which can be used whole or ground.

Cloves (Loung): An aromatic dried flower bud with a rich flavour it is used as a component in garammasala.

Coriander, Seeds (Sabat Dhaniya): Small, round creamy coloured seeds of the aromatic herb coriander.

Coriander, Leaves (Hara Dhaniya): Fragrant, green leaves of the coriander plant. Used in cooking and as a garnish.

Cumin, Black (Shah Jeera): Tiny, fragrant black seeds of the cumin plant. Used as flavouring.

Cumin, White (Jeera): These are off-white coloured cumin seeds that have a less fragrance than their black counterparts. Can be used whole or ground. Also a part of garammasala.

Fenugreek, Seeds (Methi dana): Small, dried yellow seeds with a characteristic bitter taste. Their dormant flavour becomes pronounced when fried for seasoning.

Fenugreek, Leaves (Qasuri Methi): Fresh or dried leaves of fenugreek.
Flour, Wholewheat (Atta): The most commonly used flour for making Indian breads.
Flour, Gram (Vaisin): Flour made from split yellow peas.
Food colour (Khaanwala Rang): Yellow and red food colouring powders can be bought in Indian grocery stores. There is also a tomato-coloured powder that gives a true "tanduri" look to dishes.
Garammasala: A blend of ground spices.
Ghee (Ghio): Fat made from clarified butter. Favourite medium for Punjabi cooking.
Ginger, Dried (Saunth): Can be used whole or ground but cannot be substituted for fresh ginger as the flavour is quite different.
Ginger, Fresh (Adrak): Aromatic root of a tropical plant. Can be stored in a cool, dry place for several weeks.
Gourd (Lauki): Pale green vegetable belonging to the marrow family.
Green split lentils (Dhuli mung di daal): Cook quickly and do not need pre-soaking.
Mango, Dried (Am chur): Sun-dried and powdered green mangoes.
Nigella (Kalonji): Small black tear-shaped seeds similar to onion seeds.
Paneer: Home-made cheese. See page 12.
Pepper (Mirch): One of India's most important spices. All peppercorns are green when fresh, black when dried, and white when the black skin has been soaked off. Peppercorns are used whole or ground.
Pomegranate Seeds (Anar dana): Dried seeds of a small and sour variety of the pomegranate fruit.
Poppy Seeds (Khuskhas): Tiny white seeds of the poppy plant, used as a thickening agent for gravies.
Rose essence (Kewda): Colourless liquid distilled from rose petals and used for flavouring desserts. When water is added it is called Rosewater (Gulabjal).
Silver leaves: Edible silver beaten into extremely thin and light sheets. Used for decoration.
Tamarind (Imli): Dried pods of the tamarind tree. Contain a very sour juice and sold in compressed blocks or paste form which keep for a very long time.
Turmeric (Haldi): Roots of an aromatic plant which yield a bright yellow powder. A commonly used spice with preservative properties.

FAVOURITE
SNACKS

Reshami Kebab
(*Minced Chicken Kebab*)
SERVES 4

A rather special Kebab which is not commonly sold by street vendors in India, but certain eating establishments in Punjab do specialise in them. This minced chicken Kebab simply melts in the mouth and is a real treat for the taste buds.

750g (1½ lb) minced uncooked
  chicken
1 teaspoon ground black
  pepper
salt, to taste
1 teaspoon garammasala
30g (1 oz) ground cashew nuts
  or ground almonds
30g (1 oz) fresh root ginger,
  peeled and grated
4 fresh green chillies, finely
  chopped
3 tablespoons fresh coriander
  leaves, finely chopped
2-3 drops yellow food
  colouring
1 egg
A little ghee for basting

Preparation time: 30 minutes
Cooking time: 15 minutes

1. Put the mince in a bowl and add the pepper, salt, garammasala and ground cashew nuts or almonds. Add the ginger, chillies, coriander and food colouring.
2. Whisk the egg lightly and add to the mixture.
3. Blend the mixture gently. Cover and leave for about 10 to 15 minutes. Preheat the oven to 180°C, 350°F, Gas Mark 4.
4. Divide the mixture into 8 portions.
5. Take a thick skewer, lightly oil your palm and press and spread each portion along the length of the skewer making a long kebab of about 10cm (4 inches). Rotating the skewer whilst pressing the mixture helps to make an even and smooth shaped kebab.
6. Place on a wire rack over a baking tin and roast in the oven for 8-10 minutes. Baste with the ghee and turn the kebabs once or twice so they brown on all sides.

Serve immediately with some fresh salad and Hare am di Chutney.

Unsuitable for freezing.

Previous pages: Hare am di Chutney (p.100), Reshami Kebab (p.20) and Kukkadde Tikka (p.21).

Kukkad De Tikke
(Chicken Tikka)
SERVES 4

*C*hicken, which is also known as 'Kukkad' in Punjabi language is no doubt the favourite fare of non-vegetarians. These sizzling and succulent chicken tikkas roasting in a hot tandur have an aroma that is hard to resist and are surprisingly easy to make.

60g (2 oz) natural yogurt
4 cloves of garlic, peeled and finely chopped
45g (1½ oz) fresh root ginger, peeled and grated
4 fresh green chillies, finely chopped
¼ teaspoon ground black pepper
¼ teaspoon ground dried red chillies
salt, to taste
½ teaspoon ground cumin seeds
large pinch of ground nutmeg
1 teaspoon fresh chopped mint, optional
3 tablespoons finely chopped fresh coriander leaves, optional
2 tablespoons of lemon juice
2-3 drops of yellow food colouring or 1 teaspoon ground turmeric
2 tablespoons gram flour
About 750g (1½ lb) chicken breast, boned, skinned and cubed

Preparation time: 20 minutes, plus marinating
Cooking time: 15 minutes

1. Put the yogurt in a large bowl and whisk it lightly. Add the garlic, ginger and chillies and mix together.
2. Add the pepper, ground red chillies, salt, cumin, nutmeg, mint and coriander (if used), lemon juice, food colouring (or turmeric) and gram flour to the yogurt and mix thoroughly.
3. Put the chicken into the marinade mixture, cover and leave for at least 3-4 hours.
4. Preheat the oven to 180°C, 350°F, Gas Mark 4. Place the chicken pieces and the marinade in a baking tin, taking care not to cram them too closely and roast for about 15-20 minutes.
5. Just before serving, baste them with the juices left in the tray and grill them for 1-2 minutes under a preheated grill, keeping the tray quite near to the flame to get the slightly 'charred' look which roasting in a tandur would have given. Baste with a little oil if the pieces look too dry and grill for a few seconds.

Serve hot with any chutney or simply squeeze on a little lemon juice and serve as a snack or as part of a main meal.

Suitable for freezing. Use fresh chicken and freeze the marinated pieces (up to stage 4) and finish off the cooking after defrosting.

Machi de Kebab
(Fish Kebabs)
SERVES 4

*T*his is one dish I am sure to make when giving a cocktail party. My mother used to make these kebabs as far back as I can remember and they are scrumptious. Served with any chutney or even tomato ketchup, they are a rewarding treat for very little effort.

500g (1 lb) cod steaks or any firm flesh white fish
1 teaspoon lemon juice
1/2 teaspoon ground black pepper
Salt, to taste
2 cloves of garlic, peeled and crushed
30g (1 oz) onion, finely chopped
3 fresh green chillies, finely chopped
2 tablespoons fresh coriander leaves, finely chopped
2 slices white bread made into fresh breadcrumbs
1 egg
Oil for deep frying

Preparation time: 20 minutes
Cooking time: 10 minutes

1. Steam the fish lightly and remove any skin and all the bones. Flake the pieces gently with a fork. Put the fish in a bowl and add the lemon juice, pepper and salt.
2. Add the garlic, onion, chillies, coriander and breadcrumbs to the fish and mix gently.
3. Beat the egg lightly, add to the mixture and bind it well. Divide the mixture into walnut-sized balls.
4. Heat the oil in a kadhai or deep frying pan and on a medium heat, fry the fish kebabs (balls) until golden brown. Drain on absorbent kitchen paper.

Serve hot with Anardane te Pudine di Chutney.

Unsuitable for freezing.

Machi de Kebab and chutney.

Keeme di Seekhan
(Minced Lamb on Skewers)
SERVES 4

*T*he word 'Seekh' means 'a skewer' and kebabs grilled on a seekh are termed as 'seekhan' in Punjab. The origins of such cooking may lie in the Middle East but over time it has become one of the methods used for Indian cooking.

4 cloves

8 black peppercorns

1 tablespoon coriander seeds

1 teaspoon cumin seeds

1 tablespoon white poppy seeds

30g (1 oz) fresh root ginger, peeled and grated

30g (1 oz) onion, peeled and chopped

2 tablespoons fresh coriander leaves, finely chopped

2 tablespoons natural yogurt

1 tablespoon lemon juice

1 tablespoon mustard oil

1 tablespoon dried fenugreek leaves, crumbled

salt, to taste

750g (1/2 lb) minced lamb

1 egg, lightly beaten

A little ghee for basting

Preparation time: 1 hour

Cooking time: 15 minutes

1. Place a heavy-based frying pan on a high heat and dry roast the cloves, peppercorns, coriander, cumin and poppy seeds. Stir until they are evenly browned. Remove and grind to a powder.

2. Put the ginger, onion, and coriander in a bowl, and combine with the ground spices, yogurt, lemon juice, mustard oil, fenugreek leaves and salt.

3. Add the lamb and mix thoroughly. Put the mixture into a food processor, add the egg and process until well blended. Cover and leave to stand for at least 30 minutes.

4. Preheat the oven to 180°C, 350°F, Gas mark 4. Divide the mixture into 12. Take a thick skewer, lightly oil your palm and press and spread each portion along the length of a skewer, making a 13-15cm (5-6 inch) long kebab. Rotating the skewer while pressing the mixture helps to make an even and smooth shaped kebab.

5. Place on a rack over a baking tin and roast for 5-7 minutes in the oven. Turn once during cooking.

6. Just before serving, baste with ghee and put the kebabs under a preheated grill for a few seconds. This will give a slightly "charred" look which roasting in a tandur would have given.

Serve the kebabs, removed from the skewers, with Sirkewale Piyaz, fresh salad and Naans.

Suitable for freezing.

Bhunni Kaleji
(Pan-fried Liver)
SERVES 4

*T*he cook in my parents' home often made this recipe for our Sunday brunches which we all enjoyed, but I find that it is equally good served as a snack item. This recipe can be grilled instead of pan fried, simply thread the pieces on skewers and grill under a high heat, turning frequently.

500g (1 lb) lamb's liver, cut in
   5cm (2 inch) pieces
1 tablespoon lemon juice
60g (2 oz) onion, cut up
3 fresh green chillies
1/2 teaspoon ground turmeric
1/2 teaspoon ground dried red
   chillies
salt, to taste
2 tablespoons corn oil
1 teaspoon garammasala
1 teaspoon tomato purée
2 tablespoons fresh coriander
   leaves

Preparation time: 15 minutes
Cooking time: 10 minutes

1. Wash the liver and drain thoroughly. Put in a bowl, sprinkle with lemon juice and set aside.
2. Put the onions, chillies, turmeric, ground red chillies and salt into a liquidiser and blend.
3. Add the mixture to the liver and mix thoroughly, coating all the pieces.
4. Heat the oil in a frying pan over a medium heat. Add the liver and fry for 3-4 minutes. Reduce the heat and cook until the liver is tender and brown.
5. Add the garammasala, tomato purée and coriander leaves and fry for a further 2-3 minutes. Cover and simmer on a very low heat for 2-3 minutes or until the liver is well done. Stir occasionally to prevent the mixture from sticking to the pan.

Serve with Indian bread, or simply use as a topping for mini-toasts and serve as a snack.

Unsuitable for freezing.

Paneer de Tikke
(Homemade cheese Tikka)
SERVES 4

*T*he *'tanduri' style of cooking lends itself mainly to non-vegetarian dishes. So here is a recipe for a vegetarian 'tikka' that uses paneer, a home-made cheese that does not melt when cooked. For those who do not eat eggs, omit the egg and add 1 more tablespoon each of gram flour and cream.*

500g (1 lb) paneer (see page 12)
$^{1}/_{2}$ teaspoon ground turmeric
$^{1}/_{2}$ teaspoon ground black pepper
1 teaspoon garammasala
$^{1}/_{4}$ teaspoon ground mango powder
$^{1}/_{2}$ teaspoon dry roasted ground cumin seeds
salt, to taste
1 teaspoon dried fenugreek leaves
2 tablespoons gram flour
2 tablespoons thick double cream
1 egg, lightly beaten
$^{1}/_{4}$ teaspoon ground dried red chillies

Preparation time: 30 minutes
Cooking time: 15 minutes

1. Cut the paneer into pieces 3.5cm (1$^{1}/_{2}$ inch) square and 2.5cm (1 inch) thick. Put in a shallow bowl and sprinkle with the turmeric, pepper, garammasala, mango powder, cumin seeds, salt and fenugreek leaves. Toss the paneer gently to coat well with all the spices. Set aside for 15 minutes.
2. In a bowl put gram flour, cream, egg, salt and ground red chillies. Whisk well until a smooth, thick batter is formed. Add the spiced paneer to the batter. Mix gently, coating all the pieces thoroughly. Set aside for 15 minutes.
3. Preheat the oven to 180°C, 350°F, Gas Mark 4. Thread the paneer tikkas on to skewers, leaving spaces in between each piece.
4. Place the skewers on a wire rack over a baking tin and cook in the oven for about 10-12 minutes. Turn them once during cooking.
5. Just before serving, place the tikkas under a hot grill for a few seconds to brown the edges.

Serve hot with any chutney recipe.

Unsuitable for freezing.

Paneer de Tikke and Double Roti de Pakode (p.28) with chutney.

Double Roti de Pakode
(Bread Fritters)
SERVES 4

While travelling some years ago in one of the state coaches that run frequently in and around Punjab, I came across some of the most delicious yet simple 'snack food'. Pakodas (fritters) of many types dominated the scene, but what fascinated me most were the ones made with bread slices.

180g (6 oz) gram flour
$^1/_2$ teaspoon ground dried red
  chillies
salt, to taste
$^1/_2$ teaspoon carom seeds,
  optional
2 tablespoons fresh coriander
  leaves, finely chopped
1 tablespoon warm corn oil
water to make batter
about 4 to 6 white medium
  thick bread slices
Oil for deep frying

Preparation time: 20 minutes
Cooking time: 10 minutes

1. Sieve the gram flour, ground red chillies and salt into a bowl. Add the carom seeds, (if used) and coriander.
2. A little at a time, pour in the oil with enough water to make a fairly thick, smooth batter of a coating consistency. Cover and set aside for about 10-15 minutes.
3. Cut the bread slices diagonally into triangle shapes. Put the oil in a khadai, or deep frying pan, and place it on a medium heat.
4. Take one half slice at a time and dip it in the batter. Coat thoroughly with batter and deep fry until golden. Keep the heat on medium to low so that the batter has time to cook and does not get brown too quickly.
5. Fry all the slices and drain on absorbent kitchen paper.

Serve hot with Soonth or any chutney of your liking.

Unsuitable for freezing.

Aloo di Tikki
(Potato Cutlets)
SERVES 4

Street food is enormously popular in India. The street vendor selling Aloo di tikki is the most sought after, especially if he serves a really good chutney to accompany the tikki! Here is my quick and easy way to make them. Aloo di tikki is often made with added cooked minced lamb and you can also try substituting dry cooked lentils instead of peas for a wonderful variation in taste.

500g (1 lb) boiled potatoes, mashed
180g (6 oz) peas, fresh or frozen, cooked
60g (2 oz) onion, finely chopped
30g (1 oz) fresh root ginger, peeled and finely chopped
4 tablespoons fresh coriander leaves, chopped
4 fresh green chillies, chopped
1 teaspoon garammasala
$1/4$ teaspoon ground dried red chillies
salt, to taste
1 tablespoon lemon juice
Oil for shallow frying

Preparation time: 30 minutes
Cooking time: 10 minutes

1. Put the potatoes into a bowl and add the peas, onion, ginger, coriander and chillies.
2. Sprinkle in the garammasala, ground red chillies and salt. Add the lemon juice and mix well. Gently knead the whole mixture until everything is well blended.
3. Divide the mixture into 8-10 portions. Roll each into a ball and then press lightly to form a flat, round patty. It is easier to do these against a wet palm. Shape all the 'tikkis' in this way.
4. Heat a griddle or a heavy-based frying pan on a medium heat. Use about 1 or 2 tablespoons of oil to grease the griddle thoroughly. Shallow fry the tikkis, turning them once, until they are golden brown on both sides. Keep adding the oil a little at a time while frying. Drain on absorbent kitchen paper.

Serve with either Soonth or Hare am di Chutney.

Unsuitable for freezing.

Mathi
(Flaky Pastry Savouries).
SERVES 4

*A*ll over India one can see how innovative and enthusiastic people are about 'snack' cuisine. There is a tremendous availability of food to nibble on and one of the more traditional and commonly made among them is 'mathi', a super, slow-fried, crispy savoury.

300g (10 oz) plain white flour
1 teaspoon carom seeds
1 teaspoon black peppercorns,
    roughly crushed
salt, to taste
2 tablespoons corn oil
60ml (2 fl oz) milk
60ml (2 fl oz) water
Oil for deep frying

Preparation time: 30 minutes
Cooking time: 30 minutes

1. Sieve the flour into a bowl. Add the carom seeds, peppercorns, and salt and mix well.
2. Pour the oil into the mixture, a little at a time and rub it in well.
3. Mix the milk and water together and add slowly to the flour. Knead to make a stiff dough. Use a little more water if needed. The dough should be smooth but hard.
4. Divide the dough into 12-16 portions. Roll into balls and with a rolling pin, flatten them into round shapes. They should be approx. 2.5mm ($^1/_8$ inch) thick and 6cm ($2^1/_2$ inch) in diameter.
5. With a fork, prick all over the surface of each mathi. Cover with a cloth to prevent them from drying out.
6. Put the oil in a khadai or heavy-based deep pan and place on a medium heat.
7. When the oil is fairly hot, slowly put in the mathis, a few at a time, and fry for about 1 minute or until they come sizzling to the surface of the oil. Reduce the heat to low and fry slowly until they are golden brown. Remove and drain on absorbent kitchen paper.

Serve with either Am ka Achaar or on their own.

Unsuitable for freezing. However they can be stored in an airtight container for up to 4 weeks.
Mathi and Am da Achhaar (p.105).

Samosas
(Pea and Potato Pastry Parcels)
SERVES 4

*I*f there is one snack that is universally loved across the whole Indian subcontinent, *it is the 'samosa'. The Punjabi samosa has its own little touch — the use of pomegranate seeds and its large size! Although they take a little time to make, the end result is always rewarding.*

150g (5 oz) plain white flour
pinch of salt
60ml (2 fl oz) corn oil
water to mix
1 quantity of Pea and Potato
Filling (see opposite)
flour
Oil for deep frying

Preparation time: 1 hour
Cooking time: 15 minutes

1. Sieve together the flour and salt into a bowl. Rub in the oil and add enough water to make a stiff but pliable dough. Cover with a damp cloth and leave to rest for 10-15 minutes.
2. Divide the dough into 6 and shape each into a ball. Using a little flour, roll out each ball into a thin round disc approx. 15cm (6 inch) in diameter and cut in half.
3. Make each half into a cone shape, and seal the edges with water. Stuff generously with the pea/potato filling. Moisten the edges and seal the open ends by pressing firmly together.
4. Fill the remaining cones in the same way Cover with a cloth and set aside.
5. Put the oil in a khadai or heavy-based deep pan and place it on a medium heat. Fry the samosas on low to medium heat until they are golden on each side. Remove and drain on absorbent paper.

Serve hot with either Soonth or Anardane te Pudine di Chutney.

Unsuitable for freezing.

Pea and Potato Filling for Samosas

*T*he fillings used in samosas reflect to some extent the varying regional tastes. Potato samosas are extremely popular in Punjab, with a minced lamb variety a close runner-up. Other regions use lentils and mixed vegetables as a filling for these 'pastry parcels'.

2 tablespoons ghee
1 teaspoon cumin seeds
15g (¹/₂ oz) fresh root ginger, peeled and finely chopped
4 fresh green chillies, chopped
280g (9 oz) potatoes, peeled and cut into 0.5cm (¹/₄ inch) dice
salt to taste
¹/₂ teaspoon garammasala
1 teaspoon ground pomegranate seeds
90g (3 oz) frozen peas, thawed
2 tablespoons finely chopped fresh coriander leaves

1. Put the ghee in a pan and place it on a medium heat. Add the cumin seeds and fry them until they begin to splutter and pop.

2. Add the ginger and chillies to the pan and fry for about 30 seconds.

3. Add the potatoes, salt, garammasala and ground pomegranate seeds to the pan. Mix well. Reduce the heat, cover and cook until the potatoes are tender.

4. Add the peas and mix everything well. Cover and cook on low heat until the peas are tender. Both the potatoes and peas should be soft, but not mashed.

5. Add the finely chopped coriander leaves and stir well. Allow the mixture to become cold before using for Samosas, (see opposite).

NON VEGETARIAN FARE

Makahani Murgha
(Butter Chicken)
SERVES 4

In India, this is nearly as popular as the tanduri chicken and is a must at all the Dhabas - the roadside eating houses all over Punjab. To get its orange colour, a few drops of natural orange colouring are added.

180g (6 oz) fresh tomatoes, skinned and chopped
60g (2 oz) fresh root ginger, peeled and finely grated
4 cloves of garlic, peeled and crushed
284ml (10 fl oz) carton double cream
2 tablespoons natural yogurt
$^1/_2$ teaspoon ground turmeric
$^1/_2$ teaspoon ground dried red chillies
salt, to taste
natural orange food colour, optional
750g ($1^1/_2$ lb) skinned chicken joints, leg and breast mixed
30g (1 oz) butter
1 tablespoon raisins, chopped
1 tablespoon sultanas, chopped
1 tablespoon coriander seeds, ground

Preparation time: 20 minutes
Cooking time: 30 minutes

1. Put the tomatoes, ginger, garlic, cream, yogurt, turmeric, ground red chillies, salt and the orange colouring (if used), into a liquidiser or food processor and process until everything is well blended.
2. Pour the mixture into a deep heavy-based saucepan and place over a high heat. Add the chicken pieces and stir them to make sure they are well coated. Bring to the boil, reduce the heat, cover tightly and simmer for 10-15 minutes, or until the chicken is tender and the liquid is reduced to a thick sauce.
3. When the chicken is cooked, stir in the butter, raisins and sultanas and cook, covered, for 3-5 minutes, over a low heat.
4. Remove the pan from the heat, add the ground coriander and mix well. Re-cover the pan for 1-2 minutes so that the sauce absorbs the flavour.
5. Transfer to a warmed serving dish and pour the thick sauce over the chicken pieces.

Serve with warm Naans.

Suitable for freezing.

Previous pages: Methi Murgha (p.37), Makahani Murgha (p.36) and Naans (p.92).

Methi Murgha
(Fenugreek Flavoured Chicken)
SERVES 4

*M*ethi is fenugreek, which is used in a variety of forms within Punjabi cooking. *In this recipe, either fresh or dried leaves are combined with chicken.*

125g (4 oz) natural yogurt
½ teaspoon ground turmeric
salt, to taste
750g (1½ lb) skinned chicken
  pieces, leg and breast mixed,
  cut into 12 small portions
90g (3 oz) ghee
3 green cardamoms
1 black cardamom, shelled
3 whole cloves
2 bay leaves
2.5cm (1 inch) piece of
  cinnamon stick
1 medium onion, approx. 150g
  (5 oz), grated
3 cloves of garlic, peeled and
  finely chopped
30g (1 oz) fresh root ginger,
  peeled and finely chopped
½ teaspoon ground turmeric
½ teaspoon ground coriander
  seeds
½ teaspoon ground cumin
  seeds
1 teaspoon ground dried red
  chillies
125g (4 oz) fresh tomatoes,
  chopped
125ml (4 fl oz) water
2 tablespoons dried fenugreek
  leaves

Preparation time: 45 minutes plus marinating
Cooking time: 35 minutes

1. Mix the yogurt, turmeric and salt together in a large bowl. Add the chicken and leave to marinate for ½-1 hour.
2. Put the ghee in a deep heavy-based saucepan on a high heat. Add the green cardamoms, black cardamom seeds, cloves, bay leaves and cinnamon and fry for 1 minute until they begin to splutter.
3. Add the onions to the hot, spiced ghee and cook until golden brown. Add the garlic and ginger and cook for 1-2 minutes.
4. Stir in the turmeric, coriander seeds, cumin seeds and ground red chillies and fry for a few seconds. Add the tomatoes to the pan, and cook for 2-3 minutes.
5. Add the marinated chicken and mix well. Stir in the water and bring to the boil. Reduce the heat, cover tightly and simmer for 15-20 minutes or until the chicken is tender and the sauce is thick.
6. Sprinkle with the fenugreek leaves and on a high heat, cook the mixture for a further 5 minutes until it becomes semi-dry in appearance and all the chicken pieces are well coated with the mixture. Stir well to prevent sticking and add a little water, if necessary.
7. Remove from the heat, keep the lid on and stand for 10-15 minutes before transferring to a serving dish.

Serve with any Indian bread.

Unsuitable for freezing.

Tanduri Murgha
(Baked Chicken)
SERVES 4

The most renowned and delicious recipe amongst all the tanduri dishes is the 'tanduri chicken'. Although it is difficult to produce the exact smoky roasted flavour that a tandur oven gives, it is possible to make this recipe at home. The secret to making a good tanduri chicken lies in the marinade you make!

750g (1½ lb) skinned, part-boned chicken breast pieces
30g (1 oz) fresh root ginger, peeled and chopped
4 cloves of garlic, peeled
2 tablespoons natural yogurt
2 tablespoons lemon juice
1 tablespoon white wine vinegar
1 tablespoon mustard oil
1 tablespoon dried fenugreek leaves
1 teaspoon dried mint
1 teaspoon cumin seeds
½ teaspoon ground dried red chillies
½ teaspoon garammasala
salt, to taste
4 drops of natural orange food colour
2 tablespoons fresh coriander leaves

Preparation time: 30 minutes, plus marinating
Cooking time: 25 minutes

1. Make 3-4 deep incisions in each chicken breast. Put the chicken in a bowl and set aside.
2. In a liquidizer, put the ginger, garlic, yogurt, 1 tablespoon of lemon juice, vinegar, mustard oil, fenugreek leaves, mint, cumin seeds, ground red chillies, garammasala, salt, orange food colour and the coriander leaves. Process until everything is well blended.
3. Pour the mixture over the chicken coating well. Cover and leave for 8-24 hours, in the fridge.
4. Preheat the oven to 220°C, 425°F, Gas Mark 7. Remove the chicken from the marinade and put in a baking tin and cook in the oven for 30 minutes. Turn the pieces once during cooking and baste with the juices occasionally. The chicken should be crisp on the outside and cooked through at the centre.
5. Just before serving, brush the chicken with the remaining lemon juice and place under a preheated grill for about 1-2 minutes to brown.

Serve with Tanduri Roti, Sirkewale Piyaz and salad.

Suitable for freezing. Freeze the marinated but uncooked chicken and cook after defrosting. Only use fresh, boneless chicken for freezing.

Dhaniye Wala Murgha (p.40), Tanduri Murgha and Indian bread.

Dhaniye Wala Murgha
(Coriander Chicken)
SERVES 4

*E*very year I visit my family and friends in India, and during my last trip I picked up this gem of a recipe from a rather small and inconspicuous Punjabi restaurant. This dish is absolutely delicious and the cook had no hesitation in telling me his secret which I now pass on to you!

750g (1½ lb) boneless, skinned
  chicken breasts
1 medium onion, approx. 180g
  (6 oz), quartered
8 fresh green chillies
200g (7 oz) fresh coriander
  leaves
250g (8 oz) natural yogurt
½ teaspoon ground turmeric
180g (6 oz) ghee
salt, to taste

Preparation time: 20 minutes plus marinating
Cooking time: 30 minutes

1. Cut the chicken into 12-16 small pieces and place in a deep bowl.
2. Coarsely chop the onions, chillies and coriander leaves in a food processor, or by hand.
3. Beat the yogurt gently with the turmeric and add to the onion mixture.
4. Pour the mixture over the chicken pieces and stir to coat thoroughly. Cover and leave in a cool place for at least 2 hours.
5. Melt the ghee in a heavy-based saucepan over a high heat and add all the chicken mixture. Season with the salt. Bring to the boil, mix well and reduce the heat. Cover tightly and simmer for about 20 minutes until the chicken is tender and a semi-dry gravy is formed. Stir gently during cooking to stop the mixture from sticking to the base of the pan. Do not add water as this dish is semi-dry in consistency.
6. Transfer the chicken pieces to a shallow serving dish and cover them with the sauce.

Serve with warm Naans.

Suitable for freezing.

Masaledaar Batear
(Spicy Quails)
SERVES 4

*I*n the rural areas of Punjab quails and other game birds used to be very common, but now they are a delicacy only to be found at wedding feasts. To give a special touch, this dish can be dotted with silver leaves before serving.

4 skinned, whole or halved
   quails, total weight about
   750g (1¹/₂ lb)
6 cloves of garlic, peeled
30g (1 oz) fresh root ginger,
   peeled and grated
2 fresh green chillies
¹/₂ teaspoon ground turmeric
salt, to taste
90g (3 oz) natural yogurt
1 teaspoon garammasala
125g (4 oz) ghee
1 medium onion, approx. 180g
   (6 oz), chopped
4 whole cloves
6 black peppercorns
2.5cm (1 inch) piece of
   cinnamon stick
2 brown cardamoms, shelled
¹/₂ teaspoon black cumin seeds
1 teaspoon ground dried red
   chillies
salt, to taste
300ml (¹/₂ pint) water
2 tablespoons slivered roasted
   almonds

Preparation time: 40 minutes plus marinating
Cooking time: 30 minutes

1. Prick the quails with a fork and put in a bowl.
2. Put 4 cloves garlic, 15g (¹/₂ oz) ginger, chillies, turmeric, salt, yogurt and garammasala into a liquidiser and blend well. Pour the mixture over the quails and rub all over, inside and out. Cover tightly and leave in the fridge for up to 24 hours.
3. Peel and chop the remaining garlic. Put the ghee in a deep heavy-based saucepan on a high heat and cook the onions until light brown. Add the garlic and remaining ginger and cook for 2-3 minutes.
4. Add the cloves, peppercorns, cinnamon, cardamom seeds and cumin seeds and cook until they begin to splutter and change colour. Drain, reserving the ghee and put the onion mixture into a liquidizer. Process until well blended.
5. Heat the reserved ghee and fry the ground red chillies for a few seconds. Add the marinade juices to the pan and lightly fry the quails until brown.
6. Add the onion mixture and salt and cook for 2-3 minutes. Stir in the water and bring to the boil. Reduce the heat, cover tightly and simmer for about 15-20 minutes, or until the quails are tender and the liquid has reduced to a thick gravy. Stir occasionally and add a little more water if needed.
7. Transfer the quails to a dish, pour the gravy over them and sprinkle with the almonds.

Serve with Tadkewale Chawal and Kheere da Raita.

Suitable for freezing.

Patialashahi Champa
(*Spicy Lamb Chops*)
SERVES 4

I find these tender lamb chops spiced with cumin and cooked in yogurt one of the easiest recipes to prepare. The men of Punjab are rather fond of eating this dish with drinks in the evening.

750g (1¹/₂ lb) lean lamb chops
4 cloves of garlic, peeled and crushed
150g (5 oz) natural yogurt
1 tablespoon cumin seeds
1 teaspoon ground dried red chillies
salt, to taste
30g (1 oz) ghee
1 tablespoon tomato purée
1 teaspoon garammasala
2-3 drops natural orange food colour, optional
2 tablespoons fresh coriander leaves

Preparation time: 20 minutes
Cooking time: 40 minutes

1. Put the chops in a heavy-based saucepan and place over a low heat. Add the garlic, yogurt, cumin seeds, ground red chillies, salt and ghee.
2. Cover and cook on a medium to low heat until the chops are tender and all the juices have almost evaporated.
3. Increase the heat to high. Add the tomato purée and fry the chops until brown and all the juices have evaporated.
4. Sprinkle over the garammasala and orange food colour, (if used) and fry for a further 2-3 minutes.
5. Remove from the heat. Put on a warm serving dish and garnish with whole coriander leaves.

Serve with Naans or Tanduri Rotis.

Unsuitable for freezing.

Keema Matar (p.44) and Patialashahi Champa.

Keema Matar
(Minced Lamb and Peas)
SERVES 4

I truly enjoy making this well-loved dish of Punjab because I know it has appealed to everyone who has tasted it and this leaves me with a sense of triumph, and the knowledge that good cooking does not have to be elaborate.

500g (1 lb) fresh minced lamb
1 medium onion, approx. 125g
 (4 oz), grated
30g (1 oz) fresh root ginger,
 peeled and grated
4 cloves of garlic, peeled and
 chopped
1 teaspoon ground turmeric
1/2 teaspoon ground dried red
 chillies
salt, to taste
2 whole cloves
2.5cm (1 inch) piece of
 cinnamon stick
1 brown cardamom, shelled
60g (2 oz) ghee
250g (8 oz) fresh tomatoes,
 skinned and chopped
250g (8 oz) fresh or thawed
 frozen peas
1/2 teaspoon dark brown soft
 sugar
1 tablespoon lemon juice
250ml (8 fl oz) hot water

Preparation time: 20 minutes
Cooking time: 40 minutes

1. Put the mince in a deep heavy-based saucepan on a high heat and mix in the onions, ginger, garlic, turmeric, ground red chillies, salt, cloves, cinnamon, cardamom seeds and ghee. After 5 minutes, reduce the heat to medium and cook until all the liquid has evaporated.

2. Increase the heat to high, and fry the dry mixture until it is dark brown in colour. Stir frequently to avoid the mince sticking to the pan.

3. Add the tomatoes and peas and cook for 3-4 minutes. Add the sugar, lemon juice and water. Bring to the boil. Reduce the heat, cover and simmer for about 15 minutes or until the gravy thickens and the mince is tender. Remove from the heat and leave to stand for about 5 minutes before serving.

Serve with Dhuli Mung di Daal and either Suki Bindiyan or a raita such as Aloo da Raita.

Suitable for freezing.

Raadhiya Hoya Shikar
(Pan-fried Pork)
SERVES 4

The term 'Raadhiya' is given to this dish, which means that the pork is fried to a deep brown colour in its own juices, along with various spices, and has a semi-dry appearance. Remove the whole spices before serving if you wish — although it is not done in India.

125g (4 oz) natural yogurt
$^1/_2$ teaspoon ground turmeric
salt, to taste
1 teaspoon ground dried red chillies
1 kg (2 lb) boned leg of pork, cut in 7.5cm (1$^1/_2$ inch) cubes
125g (4 oz) ghee
2 bay leaves
4 cloves
2 green cardamoms
2.5cm (1 inch) piece of cinnamon stick
1 teaspoon cumin seeds
1 medium onion, approx. 180g (6 oz), grated
30g (1 oz) fresh root ginger, peeled and grated
2 cloves of garlic, peeled and crushed
$^1/_2$ teaspoon ground turmeric
180g (6 oz) fresh tomatoes, chopped
approx. 180ml (6 fl oz) water
2 tablespoons fresh chopped coriander leaves

Preparation time: 30 minutes plus marinating
Cooking time: 40 minutes

1. Mix together the yogurt, turmeric, salt and $^1/_2$ teaspoon ground red chillies in a bowl. Add the pork and stir thoroughly. Leave to marinate for at least 1 hour.
2. Heat the ghee in a deep heavy-based saucepan on a high heat. Add the bay leaves, cloves, cardamoms, cinnamon and cumin seeds. Fry until they splutter and change colour. Add the onion and fry until golden.
3. Add the ginger and garlic cook for a minute, lower the heat and mix in the turmeric, $^1/_2$ teaspoon ground red chillies and salt. Fry for a few seconds more. Add the tomatoes and fry until well blended.
4. Add the pork and bring to the boil. Cover, and simmer gently for 15-20 minutes or until the meat is tender and the juices have almost evaporated.
5. Uncover, increase the heat to high and keep frying the meat until it is a deep brown colour and semi-dry in appearance. To stop the pork from sticking to the pan, add a little water occasionally.
6. The authentic 'Raadhiya' look will be achieved when you find that the ghee begins to separate from the frying mixture. Put into a dish and sprinkle with finely chopped coriander leaves.

Serve with hot Tanduri Rotis.

Suitable for freezing.

Saagwala Meat
(Lamb with Spinach)
SERVES 4

Spinach is extremely popular in Punjab, where it is cooked with great imagination to produce some great dishes. This recipe is one that my mother often made, which is delicious, satisfying and healthy.

60g (2 oz) ghee
1 medium onion, approx. 180g
  (6 oz), sliced
30g (1 oz) fresh root ginger,
  peeled and grated
100g (3^1/$_2$ oz) fresh tomatoes,
  chopped
2 fresh green chillies, chopped
1 teaspoon cumin seeds
2.5cm (1 inch) piece of
  cinnamon stick
2 green cardamoms
^{1}/$_2$ teaspoon ground turmeric
^{1}/$_2$ teaspoon ground dried red
  chillies
500g (1 lb) lean lamb, cut in
  2.5cm (1 inch) cubes
salt
500ml (16 fl oz) water
350g (12 oz) fresh spinach
  leaves

Preparation time: 25 minutes
Cooking time: 40 minutes

1. Put the ghee in a deep heavy-based pan and place on a high heat. Fry the onions until they are golden and remove half to use as garnish.
2. Add the ginger, tomatoes and chillies to the pan and cook for 2-3 minutes. Add the cumin, cinnamon, cardamoms, turmeric and ground red chillies. Cook for 2-3 minutes.
3. Add the lamb, salt and 375ml (12 fl oz) water and mix well. Bring to the boil. Reduce the heat, cover and simmer for 20-25 minutes or until the lamb is tender and all the liquid has nearly evaporated.
4. Chop the spinach cook it in a saucepan with ^{1}/$_4$ teaspoon salt and 125ml (4 fl oz) water, until tender. Drain and put in a liquidizer or food processor and process to a thick paste.
5. Add the spinach to the cooked meat, cover tightly and cook slowly over a low heat for about 10 minutes. Stir occasionally to prevent the sauce from sticking to the pan. The mixture should be semi-dry.
6. Remove from the heat and leave for a few minutes. Put in a serving dish and garnish with the remaining fried onions.

Serve with rice, Tanduri Roti or Naans.

Suitable for freezing.

Saagwala Meat with plain rice and chutney.

Yakhni Pullao
(Lamb Pullao)
SERVES 4

Yakhni pullao is rice cooked in a rich lamb's broth. The 'Yakhni' gives the rice a very unique flavour that is recognisably Punjabi.

500g (1 lb) boneless leg of lamb, cut into 5cm (2 inch) pieces

Piece of muslin

60g (2 oz) onion

30g (1 oz) fresh root ginger, peeled

2 cloves of garlic, skinned

2 fresh green chillies

2.5cm (1 inch) piece of cinnamon stick

4 whole cloves

1 teaspoon coriander seeds

salt, to taste

1½ litres (2.8 pints) water

250g (8 oz) basmati rice

90ml (3 fl oz) corn oil

1 small onion, approx. 125g (4 oz), sliced

30g (1 oz) fresh root ginger, peeled and grated

2 cloves of garlic, peeled and crushed

½ teaspoon black cumin seeds

2.5cm (1 inch) piece of cinnamon stick

2 green cardamoms

2 whole cloves

125ml (4 fl oz) natural yogurt

2 green cardamoms

2 whole cloves

125ml (4 fl oz) natural yogurt

2 eggs, hard-boiled and sliced

Preparation time: 30 minutes
Cooking time: 1 hour

1. Put the lamb in a deep heavy-based saucepan and stir over a high heat until browned.

2. In a muslin square, put the onion, ginger, garlic, chillies, cinnamon, cloves, and coriander and tie with a tight knot. Put the spice bag, salt and the water into the pan with the lamb. Cover and bring to the boil. Lower the heat and simmer until the lamb is just tender.

3. Remove the pan from the heat. Discard the spice bag. Remove the lamb with a slotted spoon and set aside. There should be approx. 500ml (16 fl oz) of broth.

4. Wash the rice in several changes of water, until the water runs clear. Drain the rice in a sieve.

5. Put the oil in a saucepan and fry the onions until golden. Remove half and set aside for a garnish.

6. Add the ginger and garlic to the remaining onions and fry for 30 seconds. Add the cumin seeds, cinnamon, cardamoms and cloves and fry for 1 minute. Add the yogurt, a little at a time. Add the lamb pieces and fry until browned.

7. Add the drained rice and salt to taste and fry gently for 1-2 minutes. Add the lamb broth, cover tightly and bring to the boil. Reduce the heat to very low and cook for 8-10 minutes.

8. Remove the pan from the heat and leave for at least 5 minutes. Serve garnished with the reserved onions and sliced hard-boiled eggs.

Serve with Kheere da Raita.

Gurde te Kaleji
(Pan-fried Kidneys and Liver)
SERVES 4

*T*he pronounced flavour of kidneys and liver makes this an unusual dish which is readily available in the Dhabas (roadside eating places), and restaurants all over Punjab.

125ml (4 fl oz) corn oil
1 medium onion, approx. 180g (6 oz), thickly sliced
2 cloves of garlic, peeled and crushed
4 fresh green chillies, sliced lengthwise
1/2 teaspoon ground turmeric powder
1/2 teaspoon ground dried red chillies
1/2 teaspoon ground ginger
1 tablespoon tomato purée
250g (8 oz) lamb's kidneys, skin and cores removed
250g (8 oz) lamb's liver
salt, to taste
approx. 125ml (4 fl oz) hot water
1 teaspoon garammasala
2 tablespoons fresh coriander leaves
4 lemon wedges

Preparation time: 20 minutes
Cooking time: 20 minutes

1. Put the oil in a heavy-based saucepan on a high heat and cook the onions and garlic until transparent. Add the chillies and cook for 1 minute.
2. Lower the heat and stir in the turmeric, ground red chillies and ground ginger and fry for about 30 seconds. Add the tomato purée and fry for a further 1 minute.
3. Cut the kidneys and the liver into bite-size pieces and add them to the pan. Cook for 3-4 minutes, add the salt and water and increase the heat to high.
4. Bring to the boil, reduce the heat, cover and simmer until the liquid has evaporated and the kidneys and liver are tender, about 15 minutes.
5. Remove from the heat and sprinkle with the garammasala and coriander leaves. Garnish with lemon wedges.

Serve with hot Naans. Most Punjabis eat this dish with nothing but Indian bread.

Unsuitable for freezing.

Tanduri Machi
(Baked Fish)
SERVES 4

*T*his is a dish that needs very little effort, but which produces mouth-watering results. The special 'roasted' flavour which a 'tandur' gives makes this into an exciting delicacy, but it can be done almost as well in a conventional oven.

4 fresh, cleaned and gutted trout, each weighing about 300g (10 oz)
15g (½ oz) fresh root ginger, peeled
3 cloves of garlic, peeled
2 tablespoons natural yogurt
1 tablespoon lemon juice
1 teaspoon white wine vinegar
1 tablespoon mustard oil
1 teaspoon dried fenugreek leaves
½ teaspoon dried mint
½ teaspoon cumin seeds
½ teaspoon ground dried red chillies
¼ teaspoon garammasala
salt, to taste
4 drops natural orange food colour, optional
1 tablespoon fresh coriander leaves

Preparation time: 20 minutes, plus marinating
Cooking time: 15 minutes

1. Make 2 long incisions across both sides of each fish and put in a shallow dish.
2. Put the ginger, garlic, yogurt, lemon juice, vinegar, oil, fenugreek leaves, mint, cumin seeds, ground red chillies, garammasala, salt, colouring (if used) and coriander leaves into a liquidiser and process until well blended.
3. Pour the mixture over the fish, coating them thoroughly all over. Cover and leave in a cool place for 2-3 hours.
4. Preheat the oven to 200°C, 400°F, Gas Mark 6. Place the marinated fish on a rack in a baking tin and bake for 15 minutes. Turn the fish over once after about 10 minutes to cook the fish on both sides.
5. Just before serving, put the tray under a preheated grill and brown the fish on both sides for 1-2 minutes, to give a barbecued look.

Serve with Anardane Te Pudine di Chutney and Sirkewale Piyaz.

Unsuitable for freezing.

Tanduri Machi and Machi Amritsari (p.52).

Machi Amritsari
(Carom Flavoured Fish)
SERVES 4

*P*unjabi cuisine has a limited range of fish dishes. The few that are made are usually fried and tend to be served as a snack, rather than as a main meal. The men of 'the land of five rivers' are known to be fond of 'a peg or two' and what better than a drink and some fried fish to finish off a hard days work!

750g (1½ lb) firm, white, fillet of fish, (eg. cod), cut into 7.5 x 5cm (3 x 2 inch) pieces
2 tablespoons lemon juice
salt
125g (4 oz) gram flour
45g (1½ oz) fresh root ginger, peeled and finely chopped
4 cloves of garlic, peeled and finely chopped
1 teaspoon garammasala
½ teaspoon ground turmeric
1 teaspoon ground dried red chillies
½ teaspoon ground black pepper
½-1 teaspoon carom seeds
1 teaspoon lemon juice
about 250ml (8 fl oz) water
Oil for deep frying

Preparation time: 30 minutes
Cooking time: 15 minutes

1. Place the fish in a bowl and add the lemon juice and 1 teaspoon salt and mix well. Leave to marinate for 10 minutes. Drain off all the liquid and dry the pieces well with absorbent paper.
2. Sieve the gram flour into a bowl and add the ginger, garlic, garammasala, turmeric, ground red chillies, pepper, carom seeds, salt to taste and lemon juice. Add the water a little at a time to make a batter of coating consistency. Use more or less of the water as required.
3. Heat the oil in a kadhai or deep heavy-based frying pan. When the oil is hot, reduce the heat. Dip the pieces of fish in the batter and fry 2 or 3 pieces at a time. Be careful not to brown the pieces too quickly. Keeping the heat on medium to low, fry the fish until they are golden brown, crisp all over and fully cooked.
Remove from the oil and drain on absorbent paper.

Serve with Anardane Te Pudine di Chutney and fresh salad.

Unsuitable for freezing.

Tali Machi
(Fried Fish)
SERVES 4

*F*ried fish invariably means fish fried in batter in the West, but in India, most people use no batter at all. This style of Punjabi 'tali machi' is perhaps one of the easiest and most common methods of making a simple dish which looks as good as it tastes.

750g (1½ lb) firm, white fish fillet, cut into 5cm (2 inch) cubes
2 tablespoons white wine or cider vinegar
salt
1 teaspoon turmeric
2 fresh green chillies, finely chopped
2 tablespoons ground coriander seeds, crushed or ground
1 tablespoon fresh mint leaves, finely chopped
1 teaspoon ground dried red chillies
1 tablespoon garammasala
2 tablespoons lemon juice
Oil for deep frying

Preparation time: 15 minutes
Cooking time: 10 minutes

1. Place the fish in a bowl and add the vinegar, ½ teaspoon salt and the turmeric and mix well. Leave to marinate for 10 minutes. Drain off all the liquid and dry the pieces well on absorbent paper.
2. Add the chillies, coriander, mint, ground red chillies, garammasala and salt to taste, to the fish and mix well.
3. Add the lemon juice (add a little more if desired) and let the seasoned fish stand for about 5 minutes.
4. Heat the oil in a kadhai or deep heavy-based frying pan on a medium heat. When the oil is quite hot, reduce the heat and fry 2 or 3 pieces of fish at a time until well cooked and golden brown. Drain the fish on absorbent paper.

Serve with any chutney or tomato ketchup, which is as popular in India as it is in the West.

Unsuitable for freezing.

VEGETARIAN FARE

Palak Paneer
(Spinach with Cheese)
SERVES 4

*M*any of the best-loved vegetarian Punjabi dishes are the ones where paneer is combined with a vegetable. This combination of spinach and paneer is not only highly nutritious, but is a splendid blend of taste, texture and flavour.

90ml (3 fl oz) ghee

1 small onion, approx. 90g (3 oz), sliced

30g (1 oz) fresh root ginger, peeled and chopped

2 cloves of garlic, peeled and crushed

3 fresh green chillies, chopped

90g (3 oz) tomatoes, skinned and chopped

$\frac{1}{2}$ teaspoon ground turmeric

$\frac{1}{2}$ teaspoon ground dried red chillies

salt, to taste

750g (1$\frac{1}{2}$ lb) fresh spinach, cooked or 500g (1 lb) frozen spinach, thawed

125ml (4 fl oz) milk

250ml (8 fl oz) water

180g (6 oz) paneer cubes about 2.5 cm (1 inch) in size (see page 12).

1 tablespoon thick double cream

Preparation time: 30 minutes

Cooking time: 30 minutes

1. Put the ghee in a heavy-based pan and place on a high heat.

2. Fry the onions until they are light golden in colour. Add the ginger, garlic, and chillies and fry for 1 minute. Add the tomatoes to the pan and cook until tender and well blended. Reduce the heat.

3. Stir in the turmeric, ground red chillies and salt and fry for 30 seconds.

4. Purée the spinach in a liquidiser or food processor. Add the spinach to the hot mixture in the pan and fry for 4-5 minutes. Pour in the milk and water. Bring to the boil, reduce the heat, cover and cook for about 10 minutes or until the mixture is well blended.

5. Add the paneer cubes and mix gently. Cover and simmer for a further 3-4 minutes.

6. Remove from the heat and transfer to a serving dish. Pour the cream on top and mix lightly.

Serve hot with Naans or Tanduri Roti.

Unsuitable for freezing.

Previous pages: Dum Aloo (p.57) and Palak Paneer (p.56).

Dum Aloo
(Potatoes in Rich Gravy)
SERVES 4

In the past, many invaders came to India via the Northern borders, leaving their mark on the region's cuisine. 'Dum Aloo' is an example of the rich Mughal style of cooking.

750g (1½ lb) small potatoes, peeled
Oil for deep frying
1 teaspoon cumin seeds
1 teaspoon coriander seeds
2 whole cloves
2 black cardamoms, shelled
1 tablespoon white poppy seeds
1 tablespoon desiccated coconut
pinch of ground mace
30g (1 oz) almonds, blanched
15g (½ oz) fresh root ginger, peeled
4 cloves of garlic, peeled
4 fresh green chillies
90ml (3 fl oz) ghee
1 small onion, approx. 125g (4 oz), grated
1 teaspoon ground dried red chillies
½ teaspoon ground turmeric
180ml (6 fl oz) natural yogurt
salt, to taste
300ml (½ pint) water
2 tablespoons fresh coriander leaves

Preparation time: 30 minutes
Cooking time: 45 minutes

1. Prick the potatoes all over with a fork and dry well. Heat the oil and deep fry the potatoes until golden. Remove and drain.
2. Place a frying pan on a medium heat and dry roast the cumin seeds, coriander seeds, cloves, cardamom seeds, poppy seeds, coconut, mace and almonds, until they all slightly change colour. Remove from the heat.
3. Put the ginger, garlic, chillies and all the dry roasted ingredients into a liquidizer, and process until well blended. You may need to add 1-2 tablespoons of water to produce a smooth mixture.
4. Put the ghee in a deep, heavy-based pan and place on a high heat. Fry the onions until golden and stir in the ground red chillies and turmeric. Add the liquidized mixture. Fry for 1-2 minutes.
5. Reduce the heat and stir in the yogurt slowly. Add the fried potatoes and salt and mix well. Cook for 2-3 minutes, stirring occasionally to prevent the mixture sticking.
6. Add the water and mix gently. Increase the heat to high and bring to the boil. Cover tightly, reduce the heat to low and simmer for about 15 minutes, or until the potatoes are tender but still whole and the sauce is thick. If the sauce looks dry, add a little more water and simmer for a little longer. Serve sprinkled with coriander leaves.

Serve with Bhaturas or Loochis and Naans.

Unsuitable for freezing.

Bhartha
(Roasted Aubergines)
SERVES 4

Bhartha is enjoyed by most Punjabis and falls into a class of its own. The term 'bhartha' means, to mash, and here the aubergines are first roasted, then mashed and finally seasoned. It is best to use large aubergines for this recipe.

500g (1 lb) aubergines
75ml (2½ fl oz) ghee
75g (2½ oz) onions, chopped
2 fresh green chillies, chopped
15g (½ oz) fresh root ginger, peeled and chopped
½ teaspoon ground dried red chillies
salt, to taste
90g (3 oz) fresh tomatoes, skinned, seeds removed and chopped
2 tablespoons fresh coriander leaves

Preparation time: 25 minutes
Cooking time: 10 minutes

1. Grease the aubergines lightly with any vegetable oil and roast over a gas ring or under a preheated grill. Keep turning them from time to time until they are soft and the skin is completely charred. Cool, then remove the skin and stalk. In a bowl, flake the tender roasted flesh with a fork, and then mash gently. Put to one side.
2. Put the ghee in a deep heavy-based frying pan and place on a medium heat. Fry the onions until they are golden. Add the chillies and ginger and fry for 1-2 minutes.
3. Reduce the heat and stir in the ground red chillies and salt. Add the tomatoes and cook on a medium heat until they are soft.
4. Add the aubergines and mix well. Reduce the heat, cover and cook on low for 4-5 minutes.
5. Remove from the heat and transfer to a serving dish and garnish with the coriander leaves.

Serve with any Indian bread.

Suitable for freezing.

Bhartha, Sarson da Saag (p.60), Rajmah (p.61) and Indian bread.

Sarson da Saag
(Cooked Mustard and Spinach Leaves)
SERVES 4

Immensely popular all over Punjab, 'Sarson da Saag' has certainly become one of India's favourite dishes. An integral part of the Punjabi diet, it is a robust preparation with an unusual taste. You can find mustard and fenugreek leaves in most good Asian shops.

500g (1 lb) fresh mustard leaves
125g (4 oz) fresh spinach leaves
60g (2 oz) fresh fenugreek
   leaves
4 fresh green chillies
30g (1 oz) fresh root ginger,
   peeled and chopped
3 cloves of garlic
salt, to taste
1 litre (32 fl oz) water
60g (2 oz) fine cornmeal flour
60g (2 oz) ghee
60g (2 oz) onions, peeled and
   sliced
60g (2 oz) fresh tomatoes,
   skinned and chopped
30g (1 oz) unsalted butter

Preparation time: 30 minutes
Cooking time: 1 hour

1. In a deep, heavy-based pan, put all the leaves, chillies, ginger, garlic, salt and water. Place on a high heat and bring to the boil. Cover, reduce the heat and simmer for 20-30 minutes or until the leaves are tender.

2. Remove from the heat, drain and reserve any excess liquids left in the pan. Put the cooked mixture into a liquidiser and process until well blended. Add the cornmeal to the mixture and process until fully blended.

3. Pour the mixture back into the pan, along with the reserved liquids. Place on low to medium heat and cook for 10-15 minutes.

4. Put the ghee in a small frying pan and on a medium heat, sauté the onions until they are golden. Add the tomatoes and cook for 3-4 minutes or until well blended.

5. Pour the fried mixture over the cooked 'saag' in the pan and mix well. On a low heat, let the saag simmer for a few minutes or until it is of a thick but slightly runny consistency. Put in a dish and dot with butter.

Serve with Makkai di Roti and Lassi.

Suitable for freezing.

Rajmah
(Curried Red Kidney Beans)
SERVES 4

*R*ajmah, from Punjab has acquired a reputation for being a classy dish. It is a common sight to see roadside food vendors doing good business in Punjab selling 'Rajmah and rice', a combination that is hard to beat.

500g (1 lb) dried red kidney beans, soaked for at least 12 hours, then drained and rinsed
About 1½ litres (3 pints) water
½ teaspoon ground turmeric
½ teaspoon ground dried red chillies
75ml (2½ fl oz) ghee
3 green cardamoms
3 whole cloves
1 small onion, approx. 125g (4 oz), grated
30g (1 oz) fresh root ginger, peeled and grated
90g (3 oz) fresh tomatoes, skinned and chopped
salt, to taste
250ml (8 fl oz) warm water
1 tablespoon garammasala

Preparation time: 30 minutes
Cooking time: 1½ hours

1. Put the beans in a deep, heavy-based pan, add the water and put on a high heat. Add the turmeric and chillies, cover and bring to the boil. Boil rapidly for 10 minutes. Reduce the heat and simmer for 30-40 minutes or until the beans are tender. Strain if necessary. Gently mash the beans with a wooden spoon and set aside.
2. Put the ghee in a frying pan and place on a high heat. Add the cardamoms and cloves and fry them until they begin to splutter.
3. Add the onions to the ghee and fry until golden. Add the ginger and fry until lightly coloured. Add the tomatoes to the pan with the salt. Fry until the whole mixture is well blended.
4. Pour the hot mixture over the cooked beans, mix thoroughly and increase the heat to high. Add the warm water, cover and bring to the boil. Reduce the heat and simmer for about 15 minutes or until thick.
5. Stir in the garammasala, cover and remove from the heat. Leave the pan undisturbed for at least 5 minutes before serving.

Serve with Tadkewale Chawal and Aloo da Raita .

Suitable for freezing.

Suki Bindiyan
(Sautéed Okra)
SERVES 4

*O*kras, or ladyfingers, have acquired an exotic image in the West, but in fact are one of the most commonly grown vegetables in India. Relished by both vegetarians and non-vegetarians, they are quick to cook and can be combined with a variety of ingredients to create different tastes.

125ml (4 fl oz) corn oil
1 small onion, approx. 90g
  (3 oz), sliced
500g (1 lb) okras
1/2 teaspoon ground turmeric
1/2 teaspoon ground dried red
  chillies
salt, to taste
1/2 teaspoon dried mango
  powder

Preparation time: 10 minutes
Cooking time: 15 minutes

1. Put the oil in a kadhai or deep heavy-based saucepan and place it on a medium heat. Add the onions and cook until golden.
2. Wash and dry the okras thoroughly, as any moisture present will produce an excessive amount of sticky sap. Slice or chop the okras and to the pan with the turmeric and ground red chillies, and fry for 8-10 minutes. Stir from time to time to avoid the mixture sticking to the base of the pan. Keep the pan covered as far as possible as that will help the vegetables to cook in their own juice.
3. When the okras begin to brown, sprinkle in the salt and mango powder and mix very gently with a wooden spoon.
4. Reduce the heat to low, cover and cook for 2-3 minutes. Remove from the heat and transfer to a serving dish.

Serve hot with any Indian bread.

Unsuitable for freezing.

Suki Bindiyan (p.62) and Mah di Daal (p.64).

Mah di Daal
(Whole Black Beans)
SERVES 4

Mah di Daal, with its smooth velvety texture and moreish flavour, is a delicacy that is very much a dish of Punjab. Every Punjabi restaurant, roadside eating place and food stall vendor makes the claim that this is a delicacy which they alone can make to perfection. This is my own tested recipe - dare I claim it as the best?

180g (6 oz) whole black beans
30g (1 oz) red kidney beans
1 teaspoon ground dried red
   chillies
30g (1 oz) fresh root ginger,
   peeled and chopped
2 litres (3 ¼ pints) water, for
   soaking and 250ml
   (8 fl oz)water
90ml (3 fl oz) ghee
4 fresh green chillies, chopped
60g (2 oz) fresh tomatoes,
   chopped
salt, to taste
60ml (2 fl oz) thick double
   cream

Preparation time: 20 minutes
Cooking time: 2 hours

1. Wash the beans thoroughly and put them in a deep, heavy-based saucepan. Put the ground red chillies and half the ginger into the pan with the water. Soak for at least 6 to 8 hours.
2. Place the pan on a high heat (do not drain the water) and add a further 250 ml (8 fl oz) of water. Cover and bring to the boil. Boil rapidly for 10 minutes. Reduce the heat and simmer on a low heat until the beans are soft and very little liquid remains. Remove from the heat and mash the beans roughly with a wooden spoon. Set aside.
3. Put the ghee in a frying pan and place on a high heat. Fry the remaining ginger until golden. Add the fresh green chillies and tomatoes and fry for a further 2-3 minutes until the tomatoes are well blended. Add the salt.
4. Pour the sizzling mixture over the mashed beans and mix well. Return the pan to a low heat and simmer for 5-7 minutes or until everything is well blended. Stir from time to time to stop the mixture from sticking to the pan. Just before serving, add the cream and cook gently for 2-3 minutes.

Serve with Naans or Tanduri Rotis and crisp golden fried onions.

Suitable for freezing.

Aloogobi Adrakwali
(Spicy Cauliflower and Potatoes)
SERVES 4

*T*his particular recipe is a rather special one as it is always used in the free kitchens of all Gurudwaras all over the world. Gurudwaras are the places of worship for the Sikh community whose homeland is Punjab. I have visited quite a few Gurudwaras established by Sikhs in the West and was not at all surprised to see the same 'Aloogobi Adrakwali' served everywhere!

60ml (2 fl oz) corn oil
$^1/_2$ teaspoon cumin seeds
60g (2 oz) onions, chopped
45g (1$^1/_2$ oz) fresh root ginger, peeled and chopped
250g (8 oz) cauliflower
2 fresh green chillies, chopped
90g (3 oz) potatoes, peeled and cut into small pieces
$^1/_2$ teaspoon ground turmeric
salt, to taste
$^1/_2$ teaspoon garammasala
2 tablespoons fresh coriander leaves

Preparation time: 30 minutes
Cooking time: 35 minutes

1. Put the oil in kadhai or heavy-based pan. Place it on a medium heat and fry the cumin seeds until they begin to splutter. Add the onions and ginger to the pan and cook until golden.

2. Break the cauliflower into florets and cut into medium-sized pieces. Discard the large leaves but chop a few tender ones to cook.

3. Add the cauliflower, chillies, potatoes, turmeric, and salt to the pan and mix everything well. Lower the heat, cover and cook for 10-15 minutes or until the vegetables are tender and all the juices have evaporated. Stir frequently and if the mixture becomes too dry, sprinkle over a little water and cook a while longer on a very low heat.

4. Uncover, sprinkle with the garammasala and coriander, re-cover and leave undisturbed for about 5 minutes to let the flavours mingle.

Serve with any Indian bread.

Unsuitable for freezing.

Punj Rattani Daal
(A Combination of Five Lentils)
SERVES 4

*P*unjab grows a variety of lentils and its people make full use of them. Valued highly for their nutritive contents, they can compensate very well when there is no non-vegetarian item around.

30g (1 oz) whole black lentils
(Urad Daal)
30g (1 oz) whole green lentils
(Moong Daal)
30g (1 oz) whole brown lentils
(Massur Daal)
30g (1 oz) whole yellow lentils
(Tur Daal)
30g (1 oz) split yellow peas
(Channa)
2 litres (3^{1}/$_{4}$ pints) water
90ml (3 fl oz) ghee
1 teaspoon cumin seeds
60g (2 oz) onions, chopped
^{1}/$_{2}$ teaspoon ground turmeric
^{1}/$_{2}$ teaspoon ground dried red
chillies
1 teaspoon ground coriander
seeds
^{1}/$_{2}$ teaspoon ground cumin
seeds
60g (2 oz) fresh tomatoes,
chopped
3 fresh green chillies, chopped
salt, to taste
60g (2 oz) natural yogurt
500ml (16 fl oz) hot water
2 tablespoons fresh coriander
leaves

Preparation time: 30 minutes
Cooking time: 2 hours

1. Wash the lentils in 3-4 changes of water. Put them in a deep heavy-based saucepan with the water and leave for 2-3 hours.
2. Place the pan on a high heat, cover and bring to the boil. Reduce the heat to low, cover tightly and cook for about 20-25 minutes or until the lentils are tender. Mash them lightly with a wooden spoon.
3. Put the ghee in a kadhai or deep heavy-based saucepan and place on a high heat. Fry the onions until golden. Add the turmeric, ground red chillies, ground coriander and cumin and fry for 30 seconds.
4. Add the tomatoes and chillies and fry until they are soft and well blended. Add salt to taste. Whisk the yogurt lightly and add to the hot mixture. Mix well and fry for 1 minute.
5. Pour the mixture into the cooked lentils. Add the hot water and mix everything thoroughly. Cover and cook on low heat for 20-30 minutes or until the daal is well cooked and has a creamy texture. Sprinkle with coriander leaves.

Serve with Naans or Tanduri Roti.

Suitable for freezing.

Pakorewali Kadhi (p.68) and Punj Rattani Daal.

Pakorewali Kadhi
(Gram flour Curry with Fritters)
SERVES 4

*K*adhi, *like so many other dishes, differs from region to region, with Punjabi kadhi being a rather special one due to the addition of 'pakoras' or fritters.*

For the kadhi:
280g (9 oz) natural yogurt
60g (2 oz) gram flour
1 teaspoon ground turmeric
1 teaspoon ground dried red
  chillies
salt, to taste
30ml (1 fl oz) ghee
500ml (16 fl oz) water
Pakoras:
125g (4 oz) gram flour
$1/4$ teaspoon carom seeds
1 teaspoon dried fenugreek
  leaves
$1/4$ teaspoon ground dried red
chillies
$1/4$ teaspoon ground turmeric
$1/4$ teaspoon bicarbonate of
  soda
salt, to taste
water for batter
Oil for deep frying
125g (4 oz) onions, sliced

30ml (1 fl oz) ghee
$1/2$ teaspoon mustard seeds
$1/2$ teaspoon cumin seeds
1 teaspoon coriander seeds,
  crushed
10-12 fenugreek seeds
2 whole dried red chillies

Preparation time: 40 minutes
Cooking time: 40 minutes

1. Put the yogurt in a bowl and whip lightly. Add the gram flour, turmeric, ground red chillies and salt and mix well.
2. Put the ghee in a deep heavy-based pan and place on a medium heat. Add the yogurt mixture and water and mix well. Bring to the boil. Reduce the heat to low and simmer uncovered for 15-20 minutes or until the mixture begins to thicken. Stir occasionally.
3. In a bowl, mix the gram flour, carom seeds, fenugreek leaves, ground red chillies, turmeric, bicarbonate of soda and salt. Add water a little at a time to form a thick batter. Beat well for 1 minute. Add the onions. The mixture should be fairly thick.
4. Put the oil in a kadhi or deep heavy-based pan and place on a medium heat. Drop spoonfuls of the batter into the hot oil, to make pakoras about 3.5cm ($1^{1}/2$ inch) in size. Cook until golden on all sides. Drain the pakoras and add to the simmering kadhi.
5. Put the ghee in a frying pan and place on a medium heat. Add the mustard, cumin, coriander, fenugreek seeds and ground red chillies. When the spices begin to splutter, remove and pour over the kadhi. Cover and remove from the heat. Leave to stand for a few minutes, then remove the whole red chillies and serve.

Serve hot with rice.

Unsuitable for freezing.

Kabuli Chole
(Spicy Chickpeas)
SERVES 4

*P*ick any cuisine in the world and you will certainly find some well-loved, two-dish combinations. Within Punjabi cuisine, Kabuli Chole and Bhaturas are one such popular combination.

250g (8 oz) white chickpeas

1 teaspoon salt

$^1/_2$ teaspoon bicarbonate of soda

$1^1/_2$ litre (48 fl oz) water and 250 ml (8 fl oz) water

2 teaspoons cumin seeds

30g (1 oz) dried pomegranate seeds

1 teaspoon ground dried red chillies

7 fresh green chillies

100ml ($3^1/_2$ oz) corn oil

60g (2 oz) fresh root ginger, peeled and chopped

60g (2 oz) onions, sliced

2 teaspoons dried mango powder

1 teaspoon garammasala

salt, to taste

500ml (16 fl oz) hot water

a few lemon wedges

Preparation time: 30 minutes

Cooking time: $1^1/_2$ hours

1. Wash the chickpeas and put in a large pan with the salt, bicarbonate of soda and $1^1/_2$ litres (48 fl oz) water. Leave for 8-10 hours for the chickpeas to soften.

2. Put chickpeas and water in a deep, heavy-based saucepan and place on a high heat. Add a further 250 ml (8 fl oz) water, cover and bring to the boil. Reduce the heat and simmer for 30 to 40 minutes or until the chickpeas are very soft but not mushy.

3. Place a frying pan on a high heat and separately dry roast the cumin and pomegranate seeds. Grind to a powder, sieve and discard the hard insides of the pomegranate seeds.

4. Add the ground spices and ground red chillies to the chickpeas. Cook on a low heat for 10 minutes until most of the liquid has been absorbed and the chickpeas are dark brown.

5. Chop 3 fresh chillies. Heat the oil in a frying pan and fry the chillies, ginger, and onions until golden. Stir in the mango powder, garammasala and salt and fry for 30 seconds.

6. Pour this mixture over the chickpeas and mix well. Add the hot water, cover and bring to the boil. Reduce the heat and cook for about 15 minutes or until the chickpeas have a nearly dry appearance. Put in a serving dish and garnish with lemon wedges and remaining whole green chillies.

Serve with Bhaturas and Soonth.

Suitable for freezing.

Dhuli Mung di Daal
(Split Green Lentils)
SERVES 4

*T*his simple daal is my so called 'dependable' item, especially when I am in a hurry to beat the clock and get some food ready for the family! As the lentils are split and have no skins, they are quicker to cook and also easily digestible.

250g (8 oz) split green lentils
   without their skins
750ml (24 fl oz) water
$^1/_2$ teaspoon ground turmeric
$^1/_2$ teaspoon ground dried red
   chillies
salt, to taste
60ml (2 fl oz) ghee
30g (1 oz) onion, finely sliced
$^1/_2$ teaspoon black cumin seeds
$^1/_4$ teaspoon garammasala

Preparation time: 10 minutes
Cooking time: 15 minutes

1. Wash the lentils in 3-4 changes of water. Put them in a deep heavy-based saucepan along with the water, turmeric, ground red chillies and salt.
2. Place the pan on a high heat, cover and bring to the boil. Reduce the heat immediately and cook for about 10 minutes or until the daal is soft and is reduced to a creamy consistency. The lentils should not be fully mashed or it will look like a batter.
3. Put the ghee in a frying pan and place it on a high heat. Fry the onions until light golden in colour. Add the cumin seeds and fry until they begin to splutter and the onions become dark golden in colour. Pour the onion mixture over the daal and cook for 3-4 minutes.
4. Remove from the heat, sprinkle with the garammasala. Cover and leave undisturbed for about 5 minutes for the flavours to mingle.

Serve with any rice or bread and Hare am di Chutney.

Unsuitable for freezing.

Suke Aloo (p.72) and Dhuli Mung di Daal with chutney.

Suke Aloo
(Spicy Potatoes)
SERVES 4

This simple recipe is a real treat for all potato lovers. Boiled potatoes are seasoned with some spices and then magically reach real gastronomic heights! Every region in India has its own mixture of spices to make Suke Aloo, which further varies from home to home.

90ml (3 fl oz) ghee
$^1/_2$ teaspoon mustard seeds
1 teaspoon coarsely ground
   coriander seeds
$^1/_2$ teaspoon cumin seeds
$^1/_2$ teaspoon ground turmeric
$^1/_2$ teaspoon ground dried red
   chillies
1 tablespoon tomato purée
salt, to taste
500g (1 lb) boiled potatoes
$^1/_2$ teaspoon garammasala
2 tablespoons fresh coriander
   leaves

Preparation time: 15 minutes
Cooking time: 5 minutes

1. Put the ghee in a large heavy-based frying pan and place it on a medium heat. Add the mustard seeds and when they begin to splutter, add the coriander and cumin and fry for a few seconds until they begin to change colour.
2. Stir in the turmeric and ground red chillies. Add the tomato purée and salt and fry for a further 30 seconds. Take care that the spices do not burn and keep stirring frequently.
3. Cut the potatoes into small pieces. Add to the pan along with the garammasala and mix well.
4. Reduce the heat to low, cover and cook for 2-3 minutes. Remove from the heat stir in the fresh coriander and leave undisturbed for 5 minutes for the flavours to mingle.

Serve hot with Tanduri Roti or Naans.

Unsuitable for freezing.

Bharwein Karele
(Stuffed Bittergourd)
SERVES 4

Karele or bittergourd, although quite bitter when raw, has a wonderful taste once it is cooked properly. Stuffing the gourd with various spices makes it very palatable and this recipe is used, with changes here and there, in many regions of India.

8-12 medium bittergourds, total
   weight about 500g (1 lb),
   peeled and dried
1 teaspoon salt
30ml (1 fl oz) ghee
125g (4 oz) onions, coarsely
   grated
1 teaspoon ground cumin
1 teaspoon ground coriander
$^{1}/_{2}$ teaspoon aniseed, crushed
1 teaspoon dried mango
   powder
$^{1}/_{2}$ teaspoon ground dried red
   chillies
$^{1}/_{2}$ teaspoon ground turmeric
about 250ml (8 fl oz) oil for
   shallow frying
8 button onions, peeled

Preparation time: 40 minutes
Cooking time: 30 minutes

1. Make a slit lengthwise on one side of the gourds, forcing them to open up a little without breaking into two halves. Remove any large seeds. Rub salt inside and out and leave for 30 minutes. Wash the gourds under running water and squeeze out the bitter juice which the salt helps to extract.
2. Put the ghee in a frying pan and place it on a medium heat. Sauté the onions for 1 minute and add the cumin, coriander, aniseed, mango powder, ground red chillies and turmeric. Fry for 30 seconds and remove from the heat.
3. Cool the mixture and stuff equal quantities into the gourds. Put in as much mixture as possible and then tie each one up with several rounds of thread to prevent the stuffing from falling out.
4. Put the oil in a kadhai or deep, heavy-based frying pan and place it on a medium heat. Add the gourds to the pan and fry gently until browned on all sides and tender. Cover the pan from time to time while frying, to help the gourds cook in the steam that is formed. Remove from the pan and take off the threads.
5. In the same oil, stir-fry the button onions until they are light brown and tender. Add the cooked gourds and mix gently with the onions. Return to a low heat, cover and cook for 2-3 minutes.

Serve with Tanduri Roti.

Suitable for freezing.

Lobia
(Black Eyed Beans)
SERVES 4

*P*ulses and lentils are associated with the fundamental eating habits of not only
Punjabis, but all the people of India. Generally, the daily menu in most homes is
built around the 'daal' chosen for the day, and Lobia is quite a favourite.

500g (1 lb) black eyed beans
about 1½ litre (2½ pints) water
½ teaspoon ground turmeric
½ teaspoon ground dried red
  chillies
90ml (3 fl oz) ghee
4 whole cloves
2.5 cm (1 inch) cinnamon stick
1 small onion, approx. 125g
  (4 oz), grated
60g (2 oz) fresh root ginger,
  peeled and grated
180ml (6 fl oz) natural yogurt
salt, to taste
1 teaspoon garammasala
2 tablespoons fresh coriander
  leaves, roughly chopped

Preparation time: 30 minutes
Cooking time: 1½ hours

1. Wash the beans and soak in the water overnight.
Put the beans and the water into a deep heavy-
based saucepan and place on a high heat. Add a
further 500ml (18 fl oz) water if necessary. Add the
turmeric and ground red chillies, cover and bring to
the boil. Boil rapidly for 10 minutes. Reduce the
heat and simmer for 30-40 minutes or until the
beans are tender. Gently mash with a wooden
spoon and set aside.
2. Put the ghee in a frying pan and place on a high
heat. Add the cloves and cinnamon and fry for 30
seconds. Add the onions and the ginger and fry
until golden.
3. Whisk the yogurt and salt lightly and add, a
little at a time, to the pan and keep frying until all the
yogurt is absorbed and the mixture is well blended.
4. Pour the hot mixture over the cooked beans,
mix thoroughly and return the pan to a high heat.
If the consistency is too dry, add about 250ml
(8 fl oz) hot water. Bring to the boil, reduce the
heat, cover and simmer until well blended.
5. Stir in the garammasala and coriander and mix
well. Cover, remove from the heat and leave for 5
minutes for the flavours to mingle.

Serve with Tadkewale Chawal.

Suitable for freezing.

Ghia Kofta (p.76) and Lobia

Ghia Kofta
(Marrow Balls in Gravy)
SERVES 4

A firm favourite with the Punjabi housewife, this recipe turns the humble vegetable marrow into an exquisite dish which adds interest to any meal.

300g (10 oz) marrow
30g (1 oz) onion
7g (¼ oz) fresh root ginger,
  peeled and chopped
2 fresh green chillies, chopped
1 tablespoon fresh coriander
  leaves, chopped
¼ teaspoon ground black
  pepper
¼ teaspoon garammasala
60g (2 oz) gram flour
60g (2 oz) paneer (see page 12)
salt, to taste
Oil for deep frying
For the Gravy:
60ml (2 fl oz) ghee
90g (3 oz) onions, grated
15g (½ oz) fresh root ginger,
  peeled and grated
2 cloves of garlic, peeled and
  finely chopped
½ teaspoon ground turmeric
½ teaspoon ground dried red
  chillies
½ teaspoon ground coriander
  seeds
½ teaspoon ground cumin
  seeds
60g (2 oz) fresh tomatoes
1 teaspoon tomato purée
salt, to taste
500ml (16 fl oz) water, approx.
60ml (2 fl oz) thick double
  cream

Preparation time: 30 minutes
Cooking time: 40 minutes

1. Peel and grate the marrow and onion. Squeeze out all the juices. In a bowl, mix the marrow, onion, ginger, chillies, coriander, pepper, garam-masala, gram flour, crumbled paneer and salt. Mix well and shape into 10-12 balls (koftas). If the mixture is sticky, sprinkle in a little more gram flour and grease your palms with oil.
2. Put the oil in a kadhai or deep, heavy-based frying pan and place on a medium heat. Fry the koftas in batches until they are golden brown. Drain and set aside.
3. Put the ghee in a deep, heavy-based saucepan and place on a high heat. Fry the onions until golden. Add the ginger and garlic and fry for 2-3 minutes. Reduce the heat and stir in the turmeric, ground red chillies, coriander and cumin seeds and fry for 30 seconds.
4. Chop the tomatoes and add to the pan with the tomato purée and salt. Increase the heat and fry until the tomatoes are tender and well blended.
5. Pour in the water, bring to the boil, cover and simmer on a low heat for 5-6 minutes or until the gravy begins to thicken.
6. Gently put the koftas into the gravy and simmer for another 2-3 minutes. Add the cream, cover and simmer for 2-3 minutes. Put the koftas carefully in a serving dish and pour over the gravy.

Serve with rice or bread.

Unsuitable for freezing.

Lauki te Choleyan di Daal
(White Gourd and Split Yellow Peas)
SERVES 4

The addition of one or more vegetables to lentils during cooking is very much a part of the Indian culinary repertoire. Split yellow peas are a weakness with most Punjabis, and combining them with pieces of white gourd (or marrow) creates an added interest. An uncle of mine, who was a 'pucca' Punjabi ate this nearly every day!

180g (6 oz) split yellow peas
1 litre (32 fl oz) water
$^{1}/_{2}$ teaspoon ground turmeric
$^{1}/_{2}$ teaspoon ground dried red chillies
$^{1}/_{2}$ teaspoon ground coriander seeds
60g (2 oz) white gourd (or marrow), peeled and cut into 2.5cm (1 inch) cubes
salt, to taste
45ml ($1^{1}/_{2}$ fl oz) ghee
60g (2 oz) onions, finely sliced
60g (2 oz) fresh tomatoes, chopped
$^{3}/_{4}$ teaspoon garammasala
125ml (4 fl oz) hot water

Preparation time: 15 minutes
Cooking time: 25 minutes

1. Wash the peas in 3-4 changes of water. Put in a deep heavy-based saucepan along with the water, turmeric, ground red chillies and coriander. Place on a high heat, cover and bring to the boil. Reduce the heat and cook for about 20 minutes or until the peas are soft but not mushy.

2. Add the gourd (or marrow) cubes and salt to the peas. Cover and simmer for 8-10 minutes or until the gourd is tender and the mixture is creamy.

3. Put the ghee in a frying pan and place on a medium heat. Fry the onions until light golden in colour. Add the tomatoes and fry until they are soft and well blended. Stir in $^{1}/_{2}$ teaspoon garammasala and fry for 30 seconds.

4. Pour in the water and cook the mixture gently until everything is blended thoroughly. Add the hot mixture to the cooked peas and on a low heat, simmer for 4-5 minutes. Put in a serving bowl and sprinkle with the remaining garammasala.

Serve with Tanduri Roti or Naans.

Suitable for freezing.

Paneer Mattar di Sabzi
(Cheese and Peas in Gravy)
SERVES 4

*A*ll Punjabis love this dish! The addition of this item to any menu turns a simple meal into a really special one. In taste and appearance, it is hard to find a better combination that pleases one and all.

90ml (3 fl oz) corn oil
200g (7 oz) paneer, cut in 2.5cm (1 inch) cubes (see page 12)
1 small onion, approx. 125g (4 oz), grated
2 cloves of garlic, peeled and finely chopped
1 teaspoon cumin seeds
1 teaspoon ground dried red chillies
$1/2$ teaspoon ground turmeric
salt, to taste
1 tablespoon tomato purée
150g (5 oz) fresh or thawed frozen peas
500ml (16 fl oz) water
$1/2$ teaspoon garammasala

Preparation time: 30 minutes
Cooking time: 30 minutes

1. Put the oil in a deep heavy-based saucepan and place on a medium heat. Fry the paneer cubes until light golden in colour. Drain and set aside.
2. In the same pan, fry the onions until light golden in colour and then add the garlic. Fry for about 30 seconds and add the cumin seeds. Fry for 1 minute and stir in the ground red chillies, turmeric and salt. Reduce the heat, fry for 30 seconds and add the tomato purée. Cook for 1 minute.
3. Add the peas and after frying for 1 minute, increase the heat and stir in the water. Bring to the boil, cover tightly, reduce the heat and cook until the peas are tender and the gravy begins to thicken.
4. Add the fried paneer and mix gently. Cover and simmer on a low heat for 3-5 minutes.
5. Put in a serving dish and sprinkle with garam-masala.

Serve with Tanduri Roti, Naans or Tadkewale Chawal.

Suitable for freezing.

Paneer Mattar di Sabzi.

Tooriyan
(Spicy Courgettes)
SERVES 4

*T*he Punjabis delight in preparing simple dishes and this recipe is simplicity itself! The delicate flavour of courgettes is enhanced with ginger and the whole dish is deceptively easy to make.

500g (1 lb) courgettes
90ml (3 fl oz) ghee
1 small onion, approx. 90g
  (3 oz), sliced
15g ($^1/_2$ oz) fresh root ginger,
  peeled and chopped
2 fresh green chillies, chopped
90g (3 oz) fresh tomatoes,
  chopped
$^1/_2$ teaspoon ground turmeric
$^1/_4$ teaspoon ground dried red
  chillies
salt, to taste
60ml (2 fl oz) water

Preparation time: 15 minutes
Cooking time: 20 minutes

1. Peel and cut the courgettes into 5 mm ($^1/_4$ inch) thick slices.
2. Put the ghee into a deep heavy-based saucepan and place on a high heat. Add the courgettes, onions, ginger and chillies to the pan. Cook for 1-2 minutes.
3. Add the tomatoes, turmeric, ground red chillies and salt to the mixture in the pan.
4. Pour in the water and mix everything well. Cover and bring to the boil. Reduce the heat and cook for about 15 minutes or until the vegetables are tender and all the juices are absorbed. Keep stirring from time to time to stop the mixture from sticking to the base of the pan. When the mixture is semi-dry in appearance, put into a dish and serve.

Serve with Tanduri Roti and Naans.

Suitable for freezing.

Ande di Curry
(Egg Curry)
SERVES 4

A *classic example of the heights to which eggs can be raised! Hard boiled eggs are simmered in a rich gravy to make a dish that is a treat for all egg lovers.*

200g (7 oz) onions
125ml (4 fl oz) corn oil
30g (1 oz) fresh root ginger,
  peeled and grated
2 whole cloves
2 bay leaves
2 green cardamoms
1 teaspoon ground turmeric
1 teaspoon ground dried red
  chillies
1 teaspoon ground coriander
  seeds
salt, to taste
100g (3½ oz) fresh tomatoes,
  chopped
1 tablespoon white poppy seeds
500ml (16 fl oz) water
6 hard boiled eggs, shelled
60ml (2 fl oz) thick double
  cream
½ teaspoon garammasala

Preparation time: 20 minutes
Cooking time: 35 minutes

1. Slice 90g (3 oz) of the onions and grate the remaining 125g (4 oz).
2. Put the oil in a deep heavy-based saucepan and fry the sliced onions until they are crisp and dark brown. Remove, crush and set aside.
3. In the same oil, fry the grated onions on a high heat until light golden. Add the ginger and fry for 2-3 minutes.
4. Add the cloves, bay leaves and cardamoms and fry for a few seconds. Lower the heat and stir in the turmeric, ground red chillies and coriander. After about 30 seconds, add the salt and the tomatoes. Increase the heat and keep frying until the tomatoes are well blended.
5. Grind the poppy seeds and add about 4 table-spoons of water to make a fine paste. Add this to the hot mixture, and after 1 minute, stir in the water, mixing it in well. Bring to the boil, cover and reduce the heat. Simmer for 5-6 minutes until a fairly thick gravy is formed. Add the crushed, fried onions and mix well.
6. Halve the eggs and lower them gently into the gravy. Carefully stir in the cream. Cover and cook on a very low heat for a further 4-5 minutes. Remove from the heat and leave undisturbed for a few minutes before serving sprinkled with the garammasala.

Serve with Tadkewale Chawal.

Unsuitable for freezing.

SPLENDID
ACCOMPANIMENTS

Khichree
(Rice and Lentil Mix)
SERVES 4

*K*hichree *is often associated with religious festival food and at weddings the bridal couple are usually fed khichree to symbolise their togetherness in life. A lightly spiced and delicious creation of rice and lentils, the Punjabi khichree is of a much thicker consistency than those served in other regions of India.*

180g (6 oz) long grain rice
125g (4 oz) red lentils
90ml (3 fl oz) ghee
2 bay leaves
4 black peppercorns
1 teaspoon black cumin seeds
salt, to taste
750ml (24 fl oz) hot water
A knob of butter

Preparation time: 10 minutes
Cooking time: 30 minutes

1. Wash the rice in several changes of water, rubbing it gently between the fingers, until the water runs clear. Drain and set aside in a bowl.
2. Wash the lentils in several changes of water until the water runs clear. Drain and set aside in a bowl.
3. Put the ghee in a heavy-based saucepan and place on a medium heat. Add the bay leaves, peppercorns and cumin seeds and fry until they change colour and begin to splutter.
4. Add the drained lentils and fry for 1-2 minutes. Add the drained rice and salt and fry for 1-2 minutes.
5. Add the hot water, cover and bring to the boil. Reduce the heat and cook on a very low heat for about 15-20 minutes or until the mixture is really soft. Put in a serving dish and dot with butter.

Unsuitable for freezing.

Previous pages: Khichree (p.84)and Gobiwala Paratha (p.85).

Gobiwala Paratha
(Cauliflower Stuffed Bread)
SERVES 6

*W*holemeal breads stuffed with a range of fillings and shallow fried, are a culinary speciality in Punjab. Cauliflower is a popular and interesting filling for making substantial and irresistible stuffed parathas which are a meal in themselves!

500g (1 lb) wholemeal flour
pinch of salt
water for mixing the dough
250g (8 oz) cauliflower florets, grated
45g (1½ oz) onions, finely chopped
2 fresh green chillies, chopped
15g (½ oz) fresh root ginger, peeled and grated
½ teaspoon ground pomegranate seeds
¼ teaspoon ground dried red chillies
salt, to taste
Ghee for shallow frying

Preparation time: 45 minutes plus resting time
Cooking time: 30 minutes

1. Sieve together the flour and the salt into a bowl. Add enough water to make a soft and pliable dough. Cover with a damp cloth and leave for about 30-45 minutes.
2. Divide the dough into 6 portions and shape each portion into a ball. Cover with a damp cloth and set aside.
3. In a bowl, put the cauliflower, onions, chillies, ginger, ground pomegranate seeds, ground red chillies and salt. Mix well and set aside.
4. Using a little flour, flatten and roll out each ball of dough into a round disc of approx. 10cm (4 inch) in diameter. Place a portion of the cauliflower mixture in the middle, enclose the mixture and firmly seal the edges together. Dust with flour and flatten again by gently rolling out to 15-20cm (6-8 inch) diameter discs. This must be done lightly to avoid any of the filling from spilling out.
5. Place a griddle or heavy-based frying pan on a medium heat. Put a paratha on to the hot griddle and cook on each side for 1-2 minutes. Spread 1 teaspoon of ghee on each side and gently fry both sides until golden brown and crisp.
6. Repeat with the remaining dough. Remove the hot bread from the griddle and serve immediately.

Serve with a knob of butter on top and some natural yogurt in a separate bowl.

Unsuitable for freezing.

Guchi Pullao
(*Mushroom Rice Pullao*)
SERVES 4

*T*he exquisite pullaos of India have an enviable reputation for being among the choicest of rice preparations in the field of rice cookery. To make a good pullao, one needs good rice and the Basmati variety which grows in abundance in Eastern Punjab is ideally suited.

280g (9 oz) basmati rice
500ml (16 fl oz) water
90g (3 oz) ghee
2.5cm (1 inch) piece of
  cinnamon stick
6 black peppercorns
1 teaspoon black cumin seeds
2 green cardamoms
1 small onion, approx. 90g
  (3 oz) finely sliced
2 fresh green chillies, chopped
125g (4 oz) fresh chestnut
  mushrooms, thickly sliced
½ teaspoon ground dried red
  chillies
½ teaspoon ground turmeric
salt, to taste

Preparation time: 20 minutes
Cooking time: 20 minutes

1. Wash the rice in several changes of water, rubbing it gently between the fingers, until the water runs clear. Drain in a sieve and put in a bowl. Add the measured water and soak for 15-20 minutes. Drain again, but save the water for cooking the rice later.
2. Put the ghee in a heavy-based saucepan and place on a medium heat. Add the cinnamon, peppercorns, cumin seeds and cardamoms and fry until they change colour and begin to splutter.
3. Add the onions and chillies to the pan and fry until the onions are golden brown. Add the mushrooms and fry for 1 minute. Stir in the ground red chillies, turmeric and salt and mix well. Fry for 1 minute.
4. Add the drained rice and fry gently, mixing well. Cook for 1-2 minutes or until all the grains are well coated with the ghee.
5. Add the reserved water, and bring to the boil for 2-3 minutes and then reduce the heat. Cover tightly and cook for 6-8 minutes or until all the liquid is absorbed and the rice grains are almost cooked.
6. Remove the pan from the heat and leave it undisturbed for about 5 minutes. The steam within the pan should make the rice fluffy and tender.

Serve garnished with fried onions.

Unsuitable for freezing.

Guchi Pullao and Tadkewale Chawal (p.88).

Tadkewale Chawal
(Seasoned Rice)
SERVES 4

*R*ice is eaten quite frequently in Punjab, but considerably less as compared to many other regions in India. Even so, for the daily requirements Basmati can be expensive to use, therefore a slightly cheaper variety of rice is more popular for simple rice preparations like Tadkewale Chawal.

280g (9 oz) any good quality
   long grain rice
500ml (16 fl oz) water
30g (1 oz) ghee
1 teaspoon cumin seeds
$^{1}/_{2}$ teaspoon ground turmeric
salt, to taste

Preparation time: 20 minutes
Cooking time: 15 minutes

1. Wash the rice in several changes of water, rubbing it gently between the fingers, until the water runs clear. Drain the rice in a sieve and put in a bowl. Add the measured water and soak for 15-20 minutes. Drain again, but save the water for cooking the rice later.

2. Put the ghee in a deep heavy-based saucepan and place on a medium heat. Add the cumin seeds and fry until they change colour and begin to splutter. Stir in the turmeric and fry for about 30 seconds. Add the drained rice and salt and fry gently, coating all the grains with the spiced ghee for 1-2 minutes.

3. Add the reserved water, mix well and increase the heat to high. Bring to the boil for 2-3 minutes and then reduce the heat. Cover with a tight-fitting lid and cook for 6-8 minutes or until all the liquid is absorbed and the rice grains are nearly cooked.

4. Remove from the heat and leave undisturbed for about 5 minutes. The steam within the pan should make the rice fluffy and tender.

5. Just before serving, gently mix the rice with a wooden spoon to separate all the grains.

Suitable for freezing.

Hare Matar da Pullao
(Green Peas Pullao)
SERVES 4

*O*f *all the pullaos, this is perhaps the one that is most commonly served. It looks good, tastes good and does not require much time or effort to prepare. During winter in Punjab, tender fresh peas are in profusion and all sorts of dishes are prepared with them.*

280g (9 oz) basmati or any
long grain rice
500ml (16 fl oz) water
90 ml (3 oz) ghee)
2.5 cm (1 inch) piece of
cinnamon stick
6 black peppercorns
1 teaspoon cumin seeds
2 whole cloves
1 medium onion, approx. 150g
(5 oz), finely sliced
125g (4 oz) shelled fresh or
thawed frozen peas
15g (½ oz) fresh root ginger,
peeled and grated
2 fresh green chillies, chopped
½ teaspoon ground dried red
chillies
salt, to taste

Preparation time: 20 minutes
Cooking time: 20 minutes

1. Wash the rice in several changes of water, rubbing it gently between the fingers, until the water runs clear. Drain the rice in a sieve and put in a bowl. Add the measured water and soak for 15-20 minutes. Drain again, but save the water for cooking the rice later.

2. Put the ghee in a heavy-based saucepan and place on a medium heat. Add the cinnamon, peppercorns, cumin seeds and cloves and fry them until they begin to splutter. Add the onions and fry until they are golden brown.

3. Add the peas and fry for 1 minute. Add the ginger and chillies and fry until the ginger is golden. Stir in the ground red chillies and salt and fry for 30 seconds.

4. Add the drained rice and fry gently, mixing well with the rest of the ingredients. Cook for 1-2 minutes or until all the grains are well coated with ghee.

5. Add the reserved water, mix well and increase the heat to high. Bring to the boil for 2-3 minutes and then reduce the heat. Cover with a tight-fitting lid and cook for 6-8 minutes or until all the liquid is absorbed and the rice grains are nearly cooked.

6. Remove from the heat and leave undisturbed for about 5 minutes. The steam within the pan should make the rice fluffy and tender.

Suitable for freezing if fresh peas are used.

Missi Roti
(Unleavened Gram Flour Bread)
SERVES 4

In the rural areas of Punjab, where the farmers get up very early to work in their fields, cold missi roti with some lassi is very popular. I love to eat these rotis, and their aroma always brings back memories of our old cook, who would only let me have some if I promised to drink the lassi along with them.

250g (8 oz) gram flour
250g (8 oz) wholemeal flour
45g (1½ oz) onions, finely
  chopped
2 fresh green chillies, finely
  chopped
2 tablespoons fresh coriander
  leaves, finely chopped
1 teaspoon ground cumin seeds
½ teaspoon ground turmeric
½ teaspoon ground dried red
  chillies
salt, to taste
water to mix the dough
Ghee for frying

Preparation time: 30 minutes, plus resting time
Cooking time: 15 minutes

1. Sieve the gram flour and wholemeal flour together into a bowl. Add the onions, chillies, coriander, cumin seeds, turmeric, ground red chillies and salt to the flours and mix well.
2. Add enough water to make a soft and pliable dough. Knead well, cover and set aside for 3-4 hours, or make the dough and keep in the fridge overnight to use the next day.
3. Divide the dough into 8-10 portions and shape each one into a ball. Using a little flour, flatten and roll the balls into round discs of approx. 15-20 cm (6-8 inch) in diameter.
4. Place a griddle or heavy-based frying pan on a medium heat. Put the rotis on to the hot griddle and cook on each side for 1-2 minutes. Spread a teaspoon of ghee on both sides of each roti and on a low heat, fry until golden brown and crisp.

Serve with a knob of butter on top of each missi roti accompanied with a glass of Lassi or a hot cup of Saunf Illachi di Cha.

Suitable for freezing.

Missi Roti and Lassi (p.126).

Naans
(Leavened Baked Bread)
SERVES 4

*T*he *Punjab region has an enviable reputation for having a great choice of breads within its culinary repertoire. Naans are one of its most well-known and popular preparations. Made of plain flour and traditionally baked in a tandur, they have now achieved an international status! Here is how to make them to near perfection in a conventional oven.*

500g (1 lb) plain white flour
pinch of salt
$\frac{1}{2}$ teaspoon baking powder
$\frac{1}{4}$ teaspoon bicarbonate of soda
1 teaspoon sugar
1 egg
60g (2 oz) natural yogurt
60ml (2 fl oz) milk
30ml (1 fl oz) corn oil
1 teaspoon nigella seeds

Preparation time: 30 minutes plus resting time
Cooking time: 15 minutes

1. Sieve the flour, salt, baking powder, bicarbonate of soda and sugar together into a bowl.
2. In another bowl, whisk the egg and add the yogurt, milk and oil. Whisk again thoroughly. Pour the mixture, a little at a time, into the flour and slowly mix to form a soft and pliable dough. Knead it well to make a smooth, but not sticky dough. Cover with a damp cloth and leave for 2-3 hours.
3. Divide the dough into 6 portions and shape each one into a ball. Cover and set aside for 10 minutes.
4. Preheat the oven to 220°C, 425°F, Gas Mark 7. On a lightly floured surface, roll out the balls into a tear-drop shape approx. 25-30cm (10-12 inch) long and 13-15cm (5-6 inch) wide. Sprinkle each one with a few nigella seeds and press on to the surface.
5. Place the naans on a greased baking tray and bake in the hot oven for about 8-10 minutes, or until they are lightly browned in places and puffed up into bubbles on the top.

Serve immediately with some butter brushed lightly on the top.

Suitable for freezing.

Bhatura
(Leavened Deep Fried Bread)
SERVES 4

*B*haturas have become a favourite, not only because they are a delicious bread in themselves, but served with Kabuli Chole, they have become one of Punjab's classic and reputable two-dish combinations.

180g (6 oz) plain white flour
30g (2 oz) fine semolina
pinch of salt
1 teaspoon baking powder
1 teaspoon sugar
2 tablespoons natural yogurt
1 teaspoon ghee
warm water for mixing the
    dough
Oil for deep frying

Preparation time: 25 minutes plus resting time
Cooking time: 20 minutes

1. Sieve the flour, semolina, salt and baking powder together into a bowl.
2. In another bowl, whisk together the sugar, yogurt and ghee. Pour the mixture slowly into the flour and along with a little warm water, make a soft and pliable dough. Knead well until the dough is smooth and not sticky. Cover with a damp cloth and leave in a warm place for 1-1½ hours or until it is well risen.
3. Divide the dough into 10-12 portions and shape each one into a ball. Cover and set aside for 10 minutes.
4. On a lightly floured surface, roll out each ball into a round disc approx. 13-15cm (5-6 inch) in diameter.
5. Put the oil in a kadhai or deep frying pan and place on a medium heat. When the oil is fairly hot, immerse one bhatura at a time and deep fry until pale golden in colour. The bhaturas will expand and puff up quickly, and need to be turned over only once for even cooking. They should take approx. 2 minutes each to fry. Drain and serve at once.

Unsuitable for freezing.

Tanduri Roti
(Baked Wholemeal Bread)
SERVES 4

*T*his is one of the most commonly eaten unleavened breads in Punjab, and is usually baked in a tandur. In most villages there are communal tandurs where the housewives gather with their dough and have a good gossip whilst baking their rotis! Here is an alternative method using a conventional oven to make this simple and favourite bread.

500g (1 lb) wholemeal (atta)
   flour
pinch of salt
water for mixing the dough

Preparation time: 1 hour
Cooking time: 6 to 8 minutes

1. Sieve the flour and salt together into a bowl. Add enough water to make a soft and pliable, but not sticky dough. Cover with a damp cloth and leave to rest for 30-45 minutes.
2. Divide the dough into 8 portions and shape each one into a ball. Sprinkle with some flour, cover and set aside for 10 minutes.
3. Using a little flour, flatten and roll out each ball into a round disc approx. 15cm (6 inch) in diameter and 5mm ($^1/4$ inch) thick.
4. Preheat the oven to 220°C, 425°F, Gas Mark 7 and put in a lightly greased baking tray to heat up.
5. Place the rotis in batches on the hot tray and bake them for 8-10 minutes or until they are lightly browned in places and a few bubbles appear. Remove from the oven and serve.

Serve warm, brushed with a little ghee.

Suitable for freezing.

Loochi (p.96), Makkai di Roti (p.97) and Tanduri Roti .

Loochi
(Deep Fried Plain Flour Bread)
SERVES 4

*T*he combination of loochi and some potatoes is a common preparation served by food stallholders all over Northern India. They are a particular feature at most railway stations in Punjab, where even if a train arrives in the middle of the night, you can find these being freshly made just in case you are feeling a little hungry!

250g (8 oz) plain white flour
pinch of salt
30ml (1 fl oz) warm ghee
warm water for mixing the
   dough
Oil for deep frying

Preparation time: 30 minutes plus resting time
Cooking time: 15 minutes

1. Sieve the flour and salt together into a bowl. Add the warm ghee and rub into the flour. Pour in enough water, a little at a time, to make a smooth, firm dough. Cover and set aside for at least 1 hour.
2. Divide the dough into 8-10 portions and shape each one into a ball. On a lightly greased surface, flatten the balls and roll them out into discs approx. 15cm (6 inch) in diameter.
3. Put the oil in a kadhai or deep frying pan and place on a medium heat. When the oil is fairly hot, immerse one loochi at a time and deep fry until pale golden in colour. The loochi will expand in size a little and puff up quickly while frying. Turn it over once for even cooking. They should take approx. 1-2 minutes each to fry.
4. Shake off the excess oil and serve immediately.

Serve with Dum Aloo, Suke Aloo or with any meal.

Unsuitable for freezing.

Makkai di Roti
(Corn flour Bread)
SERVES 4

Corn is grown to a large extent all over Northern India and thrives particularly well in Punjab. Using corn flour to make bread is a little out of the ordinary, but when made to combine with Sarson da Saag, one of Punjab's traditional and classic combinations is created.

500g (1 lb) corn flour
hot water for mixing the dough

Preparation time: 15 minutes
Cooking time: 30 minutes

1. Put the corn flour in a bowl and slowly add the hot water to make a fairly stiff dough. Cover and leave for 15 minutes.
2. Divide the dough into 8-10 portions and with a wet palm, knead each one well until a smooth ball is formed.
3. On a lightly floured surface, flatten out the balls by gently compressing them and turning them round and round until a flat disc of approx. 15-20cm (6-8 inch) in diameter is formed. It is difficult to roll these with an ordinary rolling pin and much easier to flatten it with the fingers. Put a piece of foil on the surface before flattening the balls and they are easier to transfer to the griddle.
4. Place a griddle or heavy-based frying pan on a medium heat and when it is hot, cook the rotis on a low to medium heat for 1-2 minutes, until brown specks appear on the underside. Turn over and cook the other side until speckled brown.
Make all the balls the same way by flattening them one at a time and then cooking them. Do not flatten them all out before hand as they will dry out very quickly and will break easily when transferred to the griddle.

Serve while still hot, brushed generously with ghee and also sprinkled with brown sugar if liked.

Unsuitable for freezing.

PICKLES, CHUTNEYS
AND RAITAS

Nimboo Adrak da Achaar
(Lime and Ginger Pickle)

*O*ne of the easiest and most economical of pickles to make, this quick recipe is used by most households in Punjab. It best made in small quantities as it does not keep for long.

350g (12 oz) green limes or
   yellow lemons
4 tablespoons salt
180g (6 oz) fresh root ginger,
   peeled
Juice of 8 limes or lemons
1 tablespoon ground dried red
   chillies

Preparation time: 20 minutes
Time to mature: 1 week

1. Wash and dry the limes. Cut into quarters and sprinkle 2 tablespoons of salt all over them. Cut the ginger into 5mm ($^1/_4$ inch) thick slices. Put the limes and ginger into a sterilised earthenware or glass jar.
2. Pour the lime juice into a bowl and stir in the remaining salt and the ground red chillies. Pour this mixture over the limes in the jar. Cover the top with a piece of muslin and tie securely.
3. Keep the jar in a warm, sunny place for 5 days. Shake once or twice daily. Remove the muslin and cover with an air-tight lid. Store in the fridge.

Hare am di Chutney
(Green Mango Chutney)

*T*here are a variety of uncooked chutneys in Punjab which could, in the Western sense, be termed more as 'sauces'. This one is based on green mangoes and coriander.

125g (4 oz) raw green mangoes,
   peeled and sliced
60g (2 oz) fresh coriander
   leaves, roughly chopped
3 fresh green chillies
30g (1 oz) onions, sliced
salt, to taste
2 teaspoons sugar
2 tablespoons water (optional)

Preparation time: 10 minutes
Cooking time: Nil

1. Put the mango, coriander, chillies, onion, salt and sugar into a liquidiser and process until smooth.
2. Add some water if you find the chutney too thick and process again for a few seconds.
3. Remove and keep in a jar with a tight lid and store in the fridge.

Previous pages: Gajjar da Achaar (p.101), and Nimboo Adrak da Achaar.

Gajjar da Achaar
(Carrot Pickle)

This simply made pickle is spiced with cumin seeds and mustard seeds and is made with mustard oil as is commom in Punjab.

1 kg (2 lb) carrots, peeled
60g (2 oz) coarsely ground
  brown mustard seeds
45g (1½ oz) ground tumeric
22g (¾ oz) ground dried red
  chillies
7g (¼ oz) ground cumin seeds
45g (1 oz) salt or to taste
30ml (1 fl oz) mustard oil

Preparation time: 20 minutes
Time to mature: 1 week

1. Cut the carrots into 5-7.5cm (2-3 inch) long sticks and dry well. Put them in a large bowl. Add the mustard seeds, tumeric, ground red chillies, cumin seeds, salt and mustard oil. Mix thoroughly. Put in a sterilised earthenware or glass jar and cover the opening with a piece of muslin and tie tightly.
2. Put the jar in a sunny or warm place for 4-5 days after which it will be ready for use.Remove the muslin and cover with a tight-fitting lid. Store in a cool, dry place.

Anardane te Pudine di Chutney
(Pomegranate and Mint Chutney)

A simple, but rather different chutney because of the use of pomegranate seeds. Besides giving a sourish taste to the chutney, they add a delicate aroma which comes through in spite of the strong minty flavour.

125g (4 oz) fresh mint leaves,
  roughly chopped
60g (2 oz) fresh coriander
  leaves, roughly chopped
30g (1 oz) onions, chopped
6 fresh green chillies, chopped
salt, to taste
1 teaspoon sugar
30g (1 oz) pomegranate seeds,
  coarsely ground
2 tablespoons water

Preparation time: 20 minutes
Cooking time: Nil

1. Put the mint, coriander, onions, chillies, salt and sugar into a bowl. Add the ground pomegranate seeds. Mix together.
2. Put the ingredients and the water into a liquidizer. Process until everything is thoroughly blended and a smooth chutney is formed. Add a little more water if the chutney seems too thick.
3. Check the seasoning, remove and put in a jar with a tight-fitting lid and store in a cool place.

Anardane te Pudine di Chutney.

Am da Achaar
(Green Mango Pickle)

*D*uring the mango season in the summer in Punjab, one can see at least two or three earthenware jars full of pickled raw mangoes maturing in the sun outside most homes. This typically Punjabi recipe for making mango pickle is one that is most commonly used in the region. Raw green mangoes are easily obtainable from leading Asian grocers, but are hard to find in Western supermarkets.

1 kg (2 lb) raw green mangoes
4 tablespoons fenugreek seeds,
  coarsely ground
90g (3 oz) aniseed, coarsely
  ground
1 tablespoon ground tumeric
1 tablespoon ground dried red
  chillies
22 g (³/₄ oz) salt or to taste
500ml (16 fl oz) mustard oil

Preparation time: 30 minutes
Time to mature: 1 week

1. Wash and dry the mangoes thoroughly. Cut into 2.5cm (1 inch) long pieces. Do not add the kernel of the raw mango.

2. In a large bowl, put the fenugreek, aniseeds, tumeric, ground red chillies and salt. Mix thoroughly and put aside.

3. Put the mustard oil in a pan and place it on a medium heat. Bring to smoking point, remove from the heat and leave to cool completely.

4. Pour half the oil onto the mixed spices and stir well. Add the pieces of mango and mix thoroughly, coating all the pieces with the spice mixture. Stir in the remaining oil.

5. Transfer to a sterilised earthenware (preferably) or glass jar and cover securely with a piece of muslin tied around the opening of the jar.

6. Keep the jar in a warm and sunny place for 4-5 days. Remove the piece of muslin and cover with an airtight lid.

7. The pickle will be ready to eat within a week, but its taste improves if left for 2-3 weeks. Store in a cool, dry place.

Khatta Mitha Achaar
(Sweet and Sour Mixed Vegetable)

*T*his sweet and sour type of pickle is well known as a speciality of Punjabis who often eat it as a side vegetable. It keeps well for a year or more and so is made in large quantities in Punjabi homes.

350g (12 oz) cauliflower, cut in small florets

325g (11 oz) turnips, peeled and cut in 2.5mm ($^1/_8$ inch) slices

280g (9 oz) carrots, peeled and cut into 5cm (2 inch) sticks

60g (2 oz) fresh root ginger

45g ($1^1/_2$ oz) cloves of garlic

375ml (12 fl oz) mustard oil

2 bay leaves

45g ($1^1/_2$ oz) coarsely ground mustard seeds

30g (1 oz) ground dried red chillies

22g ($^3/_4$ oz) salt, or to taste

15g ($^1/_2$ oz) cumin seeds

22g ($^3/_4$ oz) garammasala

pinch of grated nutmeg

180ml (6 fl oz) malt vinegar

180ml (6 fl oz) molasses or dark brown sugar

Preparation time: 30 minutes
Cooking time: 10 minutes

1. Wash the cauliflower, turnips and carrots and dry them completely in the sun, or in a warm place for 24 hours.

2. Peel the ginger and garlic. Grind them to a paste.

3. Put the oil in a kadhai or pan and place it on a medium heat. Bring to smoking point, reduce the heat to low and add the bay leaves, ginger and garlic paste. Sauté until light golden and add the mustard seeds, ground red chillies, salt, cumin seeds, garammasala and nutmeg. Mix gently and add the dried vegetables. Stir well and cook for 4-5 minutes on a low heat. Remove from the heat and leave aside to cool.

4. Put the vinegar in a saucepan and place it on a high heat. Bring to the boil, reduce the heat and add the molasses or sugar. Cook until the molasses or sugar is completely dissolved and the syrup thickens slightly. Remove from the heat and cool.

5. Pour the syrup over the vegetables and mix thoroughly. Put in a sterilised earthenware or glass jar. Tie a piece of muslin tightly over the opening of the jar. Keep in a warm and sunny place for 4 to 5 days to mature.

6. Remove the muslin and cover with a tight-fitting lid. The pickle should be ready to eat within 2 weeks. Store in a cool, dry place.

Sirkewale Piyaz
(Onions in Vinegar)

This very quickly made onion relish is usually served with grilled meats, but is also suitable served as part of a main meal. Tomato food colouring powder is not made from tomatoes, but refers to the type of red colour it produces. It is a cross between red and orange and is a true 'tanduri' red. It can be obtained from Indian grocers.

180g (6 oz) onions
6 tablespoons malt vinegar
1/4 teaspoon ground dried red
   chillies
1/2 teaspoon salt, or to taste
pinch of tomato food colouring
   powder

Preparation time: 10 minutes
Cooking time: Nil

1. Peel and finely slice the onions. Separate the slices into rings and put in a small saucepan.
2. Place the saucepan on a medium heat. Add the vinegar, ground red chillies, salt and colouring. Stir well and bring to the boil. Remove from the heat immediately. Cover and leave to cool.
3. The onions should have slightly softened and be lightly coloured. Transfer to a serving bowl and eat within a day.

Aloo da Raita
(Potatoes in Yogurt)

The use of yogurt is an integral part of Indian cuisine. Some form of yogurt is generally served with most meals and when another raw or cooked ingredient is added to natural yogurt, it is termed a 'raita'.

180g (6 oz) boiled potatoes
300ml (10 fl oz) natural yogurt
salt, to taste
1/4 teaspoon ground black
   pepper
1/4 teaspoon cumin seeds
a pinch of ground dried red
   chillies

Preparation time: 25 minutes
Cooking time: Nil

1. Cut the potatoes into 1cm (1/2 inch) cubes.
2. Put the yogurt in a serving bowl and whisk with the salt and pepper until smooth and creamy. Add the potatoes and mix gently.
3. Dry roast the cumin seeds in a pan on a high heat until they begin to splutter. Remove and grind to a powder. Sprinkle the ground cumin seeds and ground red chillies over the raita. Chill and serve.

Aloo da Raita and Sirkewale Piyaz.

Soonth
(Dried Mango and Ginger Sauce)

*D*ried green mango and ginger powder are widely used ingredients for chutneys in Northern India. They are used to make this wonderful 'Soonth', which makes an ideal partner for most snacks such as Samosas and Aloo di Tikki.

150g (5 oz) molasses or dark
  brown sugar
150ml (5 fl oz) hot water
60g (2 oz) dried ground green
  mango
1 teaspoon salt, or to taste
$^1/_2$ teaspoon ground dried red
  chillies
$^1/_2$ teaspoon dry roasted cumin
  seeds
$^1/_2$ teaspoon ground black
  pepper
$^1/_2$ teaspoon dried ground
  ginger
1 drop red food colouring

Preparation time: 15 minutes
Cooking time: 10 minutes

1. Put the molasses and hot water in a saucepan and place on a medium heat. Cook until the molasses are completely dissolved and the syrup is slightly thick.
2. Reduce the heat and add the mango powder. Cook on low heat for 1-2 minutes. Remove from the heat and add the salt, ground red chillies, cumin seeds, black pepper and ginger. Mix thoroughly. If the mixture appears too thick, dilute with a little hot water and cook on low heat for a further 2-3 minutes.
3. Remove from the heat and add the red food colouring to give a brick-red colour. Check the seasoning and adjust the salt and sugar according to taste. The mixture should be of a sauce-like consistency
4. Cool and keep in a sterilised container in the fridge for up to 5 days.

Kheere da Raita
(Cucumber in Yogurt)
SERVES 4

*P*unjabis are great consumers of all forms of milk, with natural yogurt being one of their favourites. To vary the taste of natural yogurt, grated cucumber, with its refreshing taste, is often added and becomes an ideal accompaniment for most meals.

180g (6 oz) cucumber
300ml (10 fl oz) natural yogurt
^{1}/$_2$ teaspoon salt, or to taste
^{1}/$_4$ teaspoon ground dried red
   chillies
pinch of ground black pepper

Preparation time: 20 minutes
Cooking time: Nil

1. Wash and grate the cucumber with its skin. Squeeze out as much water as possible from the grated cucumber.
2. Put the yogurt in a serving bowl and whisk with the salt and ground red chillies until smooth and creamy.
3. Add the cucumber and mix well. Sprinkle the ground black pepper on top, chill and serve.

Lauki da Raita
(Grated White Gourd in Yogurt)
SERVES 4

*T*here are no set guidelines as to which raita should be served with which meal. They are interchangeable according to one's own preference, but remember that no meal is complete without a yogurt dish of some sort to accompany it!

180g (6 oz) white gourd, or
   carrot
300ml (10 fl oz) natural yogurt
^{1}/$_2$ teaspoon salt or to taste
^{1}/$_4$ teaspoon ground black
   pepper

Preparation time: 20 minutes
Cooking time: Nil

1. Peel the white gourd and grate coarsely. Put in a bowl and add sufficient boiling water to cover it completely. Allow to stand for 5-7 minutes. Drain the water and squeeze out any extra liquid from the vegetable. Put to one side to cool.
2. Put the yogurt in a serving bowl and whisk with the salt and pepper until smooth and creamy.
3. Add the cooked white gourd and mix well. Chill

SWEETS

Mithe Chawal
(Sweet Saffron Rice)
SERVES 4

*D*esserts made with rice are popular in Punjab and this particularly unusual version of rice is a speciality prepared for important occasions.

250g (8 oz) basmati rice
400ml (14 fl oz) water
90g (3 oz) ghee
3 green cardamoms
4 whole cloves
1/2 teaspoon saffron
1 tablespoon hot water
180g (6 oz) sugar
30g (1 oz) sultanas
30g (1 oz) slivered almonds
30g (1 oz) shelled pistachios,
   roughly chopped
2-3 drops rose essence
3-4 silver leaves

Preparation time: 20 minutes
Cooking time: 30 minutes

1. Wash the rice in several changes of water, until the water runs clear. Soak in a bowl with 400 ml (14 fl oz) of water and leave for 15-20 minutes. Drain and reserve the water for cooking the rice later.
2. Put the ghee in a deep heavy-based saucepan and place it on a medium heat. Add the whole cardamoms and cloves and fry until they change colour and begin to splutter.
3. Add the drained rice and fry for 3-4 minutes. Pour in the reserved water and bring to the boil. Reduce the heat and cook until the rice is tender.
4. Add the saffron to the hot water and crush gently. Leave to stand 1-2 minutes.
5. Add the sugar and saffron to the rice and stir until the sugar has dissolved.
6. Preheat the oven to 120°C, 250°F, Gas Mark 1/2 Soak the sultanas in a little hot water for 5 minutes, then drain.
7. Add the sultanas and half the amount of almonds and pistachios to the pan and stir gently. Add the rose essence and mix gently.
8. Transfer the rice to an ovenproof dish, sprinkle with the remaining nuts, cover and bake in the oven for about 15-20 minutes.

Serve hot, decorated with the silver leaves.

Unsuitable for freezing.

Previous pages: Gulab Jamun (p.113) and Mithe Chawal (p.112).

Gulab Jamun
(Milk Balls in Syrup)
SERVES 4

*M*ost *Indians have a sweet tooth and like to end their meals with a dessert which is usually milk-based. Gulab jamuns are easy to make with powdered milk and although they are a little on the sweet side, they are a delightful treat.*

500ml (16 fl oz) water
250g (8 oz) sugar
4 green cardamoms
1/2 teaspoon rose essence
60g (2 oz) self-raising flour
1 teaspoon semolina
250g (8 oz) full cream milk
  powder
pinch of saffron, crushed
30g (1 oz) butter
125g (4 oz) paneer,
  (see page 12)
a little warm milk for mixing
  the dough
Oil for deep frying

Preparation time: 40 minutes
Cooking time: 20 minutes

1. Put the water, sugar and 2 crushed cardamoms in a pan and place on a medium heat. Boil until the mixture is the consistency of a light syrup. Remove the cardamom skins and leave the syrup to cool. Add the rose essence, cover and set aside.
2. Sieve the flour, semolina, and milk powder into a bowl.
3. Shell the remaining cardamoms, crush the seeds and add to the flour with the saffron. Rub in the butter and crumbled paneer and mix well.
4. Slowly add enough milk to make a soft, smooth and pliable dough. Cover and leave for 30 minutes.
5. Divide the dough into 12 and roll into balls.
6. Put the oil in a kadhai or deep heavy-based pan and place it on a medium heat. Gently and slowly fry the balls until golden brown and thoroughly cooked.
7. Remove the balls with a slotted spoon, shake off any excess oil and put them into the syrup. Place the pan on a medium heat and bring to the boil. Remove the pan from the heat, cover tightly and leave for 3-4 hours for the syrup to be absorbed by the milk balls.

Serve hot or cold as a dessert on their own, or with double cream.

Suitable for freezing.

Kheer
(Rich Rice Pudding)
SERVES 4

This is a traditional Indian rice pudding which is quite different from the Western rice pudding. In Punjab, where dairy products are plentiful, it is very popular.

60g (2 oz) basmati rice
125ml (4 fl oz) water
1 litre (32 fl oz) full cream milk
180g (6 oz) sugar
3 green cardamoms
30g (1 oz) slivered almonds
1 teaspoon rosewater

Preparation time: 15 minutes
Cooking time: 1 hour

1. Wash the rice in several changes of water. Drain well. Add 125ml (4 fl oz) of water and cook in a pan until all the water is absorbed and the rice is soft.
2. Put the milk in a heavy-based pan and bring to the boil. Reduce the heat and add the cooked rice. Simmer on a low heat for about 30 to 45 minutes or until creamy. Stir frequently to prevent the mixture from sticking. Scrape off all the mixture that sticks to the sides of the pan and add to the thickening kheer.
3. Add the sugar and stir until dissolved. Remove from the heat.
4. Peel the cardamoms and crush the seeds. Add the cardamom seeds, almonds and rosewater to the pan and mix well. Put in a dish and serve.

Serve hot or cold on its own or to accompany Malaipurras.

Suitable for freezing.

Kheer and Gajrela (p.116).

Gajrela
(*Carrot and Milk Pudding*)
SERVES 4

*T*his is one of the choicest sweet dishes of Northern India. In Punjab, it is generally associated with the winter months when a variety of carrots grow profusely. Cooked with milk, sugar, paneer and ghee, 'Gajrela' is a sumptuous dessert.

500ml (16 fl oz) full cream
  milk
500g (1 lb) carrots, scraped and
  finely grated
90g (3 oz) sugar
4 tablespoons ghee
3 green cardamoms
60g (2 oz) paneer, (see page 12)
1 tablespoon slivered almonds
1 tablespoon chopped pistachio
  nuts
1 tablespoon raisins
2-3 silver leaves (optional)

Preparation time: 30 minutes
Cooking time: 45 minutes

1. Put the milk in a deep heavy-based saucepan and place on a high heat. Bring to the boil, lower the heat and add the carrots. Cook until the carrots are soft and most of the liquid has evaporated.
2. Stir in the sugar and cook for 4-5 minutes or until the sugar has dissolved. Stir frequently. Add the ghee and cook for 5-6 minutes.
3. Shell the cardamoms, remove the seeds and grind coarsely. Add to the pan and mix well.
4. Crumble the paneer roughly. Add to the pan and mix thoroughly. Cook for 2-3 minutes. The whole mixture should be fairly dry but moist in texture.
5. Add the almonds, pistachios and raisins. Mix well, cover and remove from the heat. Transfer to a shallow serving dish. Decorate with silver leaves, if liked, and always serve hot.

Serve as a dessert on special occasions.

Suitable for freezing.

Suki Seviyan
(Sweet Vermicelli)
SERVES 4

*I*n India, there are very few preparations which call for the use of vermicelli, but this simple dessert is a popular one in Punjab. Traditionally, vermicelli was made at home, but now a variety of vermicelli can be bought. The one I like to use is the slightly thicker kind, which also comes slightly roasted and is absolutely right for the following recipe.

90g (3 oz) ghee
2 green cardamoms
180g (6 oz) vermicelli
1 tablespoon chopped cashew nuts
1 tablespoon chopped almonds
1 tablespoon sultanas
90g (3 oz) sugar
180ml (6 fl oz) warm water

Preparation time: 15 minutes
Cooking time: 30 minutes

1. Put the ghee in a heavy-based pan and place on a medium heat. Shell the cardamoms, crush the seeds and add to the ghee. Fry for a few seconds.
2. Add the vermicelli and on a low heat, fry until golden brown. This must be done slowly whilst constantly stirring the vermicelli for even browning.
3. Add the cashew nuts, almonds and sultanas and fry for 30-60 seconds.
4. Add the sugar and warm water. Mix gently to avoid breaking up the vermicelli. Cover, and bring to the boil. Reduce the heat and simmer until all the liquid is absorbed and the vermicelli is tender. Be careful not to overcook. Increase the heat and dry off the liquids quickly if the vermicelli looks like being overcooked.

Serve warm sprinkled with soft brown sugar.

Unsuitable for freezing.

Malaipura
(Creamy Pancake)
SERVES 4

*P*urras are a sweet which are traditionally made during the rainy season in Punjab. Somehow, the dark clouds and the thundering rains that beat down ferociously puts one in a mood to have something nice, warm and filling - and purras are perfect!

150g (5 oz) plain white flour
180ml (6 fl oz) milk
180ml (6 fl oz) double cream
150g (5 oz) sugar
180ml (6 fl oz) water
1/2 teaspoon aniseed, crushed
1/4 teaspoon saffron, crushed
1/2 teaspoon rosewater
Oil for shallow frying
2 tablespoons mixed chopped
   nuts

Preparation time: 45 minutes
Cooking time: 20 minutes

1. Put the flour in a bowl. Mix together the milk and cream and add, a little at a time, to the flour. Stir constantly until the mixture becomes a creamy batter of pouring consistency. Add a little more or less liquid as needed. Cover and leave for 30 minutes. Mix well just before use.
2. Put the sugar and water in a pan and place it on a medium heat. Bring to the boil, add the aniseed, lower the heat and simmer until a thick syrup is formed.
3. Remove from the heat, add the saffron and rose-water and set aside.
4. Place a heavy-based frying pan on a medium heat and add enough oil to coat the surface. Pour a tablespoon of batter into the pan and gently swirl it into a circle of about 10cm (4 inches). Lower the heat and fry for about 30 seconds or until the underside is golden brown. Turn over and fry gently for 1 minute or until golden brown. Repeat using the remaining batter to make more pancakes.
5. Arrange the malaipurras on a serving dish, pour the syrup all over and decorate with chopped nuts. Serve hot.

Unsuitable for freezing.

Malaipura and Am di Kulfi (p. 120).

Am di Kulfi
(Homemade Mango Ice Cream)
MAKES 6

*T*his creamy, rich and extravagant dessert is traditionally frozen and served in *'kulfi-de-saanche'*. These are small, conical-shaped aluminium moulds that are very inexpensive and available at most Asian supermarkets. A delightful and refreshing change from the usual ice creams, here is a typically Punjabi recipe for mango kulfi.

500g (1 lb) rabhri (see below)
125g (4 oz) fresh mango purée

Preparation time: 15 minutes
Cooking time: 1 hour

1. Put the rabhri in a bowl and when cool add the mango purée. Mix well and fill 6 kulfi moulds or an ice cream mould or foil container and freeze.
2. A few minutes before serving, remove from the freezer and take out of the moulds. If made in one large mould, cut into 2.5cm (1 inch) thick slices.

Serve with slices of fresh mango.

Suitable for freezing.

Rabhri
(Dried Fresh Milk Pudding)

1½ litres (48 fl oz) full cream milk
150g (5 oz) sugar

1. Put the milk in a deep heavy-based pan on a high heat. Bring to the boil, reduce the heat to low and simmer until the milk is reduced to ¼ of its original volume. It is important to stir the milk constantly for the first 15 minutes and then at 2-3 minute intervals. Take care that it does not stick to the base of the pan and does not boil over. Adjust the heat accordingly.
2. When the mixture is creamy, and of a granular-like consistency, add the sugar and stir until dissolved. Remove the pan from the heat. Cool and use as required for Am di Kulfi.

Phirni
(Ground Rice Pudding)
SERVES 4

A wonderful, creamy ground rice pudding that tastes superb and is also surprisingly simple to make. A common preparation in most Punjabi households, it is traditionally served in earthenware bowls called 'shikoras.'

45g (1¹/₂ oz) basmati rice
1 litre (32 fl oz) full cream milk
30g (1 oz) ground cashew nuts,
  optional
180g (6 oz) sugar
¹/₂ teaspoon saffron
1 tablespoon milk
30g (1 oz) slivered almonds
15g (¹/₂ oz) shelled pistachios,
  roughly chopped
1 teaspoon rosewater
4 silver leaves

Preparation time: 30 minutes
Cooking time: 15 minutes

1. Wash the rice in several changes of water, until the water runs clear. Soak in a bowl with sufficient water to cover. Leave for at least 30 minutes.
2. Drain the rice and put it in a liquidizer. Add 1-2 tablespoons of water and process until the rice is ground to a fine paste.
3. In a pan, mix the rice paste with 1 litre (32 fl oz) milk and cook on a medium heat, stirring constantly, until creamy and smooth.
4. Reduce the heat and add the cashew nuts (if used) and sugar. Stir until the mixture begins to thicken.
5. Crush the saffron and mix with 1 tablespoon of milk. Add the saffron and half the almonds and pistachios to the rice. Stir well and remove from the heat and cool.
6. Mix in the rosewater and pour into individual bowls and chill in the fridge until set. Serve decorated with silver leaves and sprinkled with remaining nuts.

Unsuitable for freezing.

DRINKS

Jaljeera
(*Cumin Flavoured Appetiser*)
SERVES 4

In this recipe, the flavours of cumin mingle with tamarind, mint and ginger to produce a distinctive and aromatic drink.

2 litres (3 pints) water
60g (2 oz) tamarind paste
30g (1 oz) ground fresh or
  dried mint leaves
1 tablespoon ground cumin
  seeds
1 tablespoon dark brown sugar
1 teaspoon rock salt
$^1/_2$ teaspoon ground black
  pepper
salt, to taste
30g (1 oz) fresh root ginger,
  peeled and grated
a few fresh mint leaves

1. Put the water in a jug and stir in the tamarind and mix well. Add the mint, cumin seed, sugar, rock salt, pepper and salt to taste and mix until the sugar dissolves. Add the ginger and leave covered for 2-3 hours.
2. Strain through a muslin cloth. Check the seasoning. Chill and then add mint leaves and ice cubes to serve.

Shakanjawi
(*Sweet and Sour Fresh Lime Drink*)
SERVES 4

Shakanjawi is an incredibly easy drink to make and its refreshing lemony flavour has a remarkable cooling effect.

1 litre (32 fl oz) water
75ml ($2^1/_2$ fl oz) juice from
  green limes
60g (2 oz) sugar
$^1/_2$ teaspoon salt or to taste
a pinch of freshly milled black
  pepper
4-6 fresh mint leaves

1. Put the water in a jug and mix in the lime juice. Stir in the sugar, salt and pepper and mix until the sugar is fully dissolved.
2. Serve chilled with mint leaves and ice cubes.

Previous pages: Lassi (p.126), Kanji (p.125), Jaljeera, Saunf Illachi di cha (p.126), Malaiwala Garam Dudh (p.125) and Shakanjawi .

Kanji
(Spiced Carrot Drink)
SERVES 4

*K*anji is an unusual drink which is commonly made in the rural areas of Punjab. It is made with deep-coloured carrots and a touch of mustard and pepper.

2 litres (3 pints) warm water
1 tablespoon coarsely ground
   mustard seeds
1 tablespoon coarsely ground
   black pepper
1/2 teaspoon ground dried red
   chillies
2 medium carrots, peeled and
   cut into sticks
1 teaspoon salt, or to taste
2 medium cooked, peeled and
   quartered beetroots

Preparation time: 30 minutes
Time to mature: 1 week

1. Pour the water into a jar with a tight-fitting lid. Add the mustard and mix well. Put on the lid and keep in a warm place for 48 hours. Shake the jar 3 times during this period.
2. Add the pepper and ground red chillies. Mix well, replace the lid and keep in a warm place for 12 hours. Shake once in between.
3. Add the carrots and the salt. Shake the contents of the jar vigorously. Leave for 12 hours.
4. Add the beetroot and leave the jar in a warm (preferably sunny) place for 2-3 days to mature.
5. Keep the jar in the fridge and serve chilled. Mix well and strain before serving. Add 2-3 pieces of carrot to the glass with the kanji.

Malaiwala Garam Dudh
(Creamy Hot Milk)
SERVES 4

*M*alaiwala dudh is the kind of hot milk drink that is often bought at the 'halwais' or sweetmeat sellers who establish themselves in every market place in Punjab.

2 litres (3 pints) full cream milk
4 tablespoons sugar, or to taste
4 tablespoons extra thick cream

1. Put the milk in a kadhai or heavy-based pan and place on a high heat. Bring to the boil, reduce the heat to low and simmer until the milk reduces to at least 3/4 of the original amount.
2. Add the sugar and stir until completely dissolved. Pour while hot into thick glass tumblers. Add a tablespoon of cream and let it float on top of each glass.

Lassi
(Savoury Buttermilk)
SERVES 4

*L*assi *is an age-old beverage of India which has stood the test of time and is a thirst quencher of enormous popularity amongst all Indians. In Punjab it is 'the drink' of the people, which is served with a meal or on its own at any time of the day.*

250ml (8 fl oz) natural yogurt
salt, to taste
1 litre (32 fl oz) water
a few ice-cubes
a pinch of freshly milled black
  pepper, optional

1. Put the yogurt, salt and water in a blender. Process until everything is whisked well. Check the seasoning. Pour the lassi into a jug and leave in the fridge to chill.
2. To serve, put some ice cubes in a glass, top up with lassi and sprinkle with a little pepper if desired.

Saunf Illachi di Cha
(Spice Flavoured Tea)
SERVES 4

*A*n infusion of tea leaves, green cardamoms and aniseeds, this is a sweet, strong tea *which is an exciting and highly aromatic drink.*

1.8 litres (2 pints) water
3 tablespoons strong tea leaves
2 green cardamoms
1 tablespoon aniseeds
3 tablespoons sugar
180ml (6 fl oz) full cream milk

1. Put the water in a saucepan and bring to the boil. Reduce the heat and add the tea leaves, whole cardamoms and aniseeds and simmer for 2-3 minutes.
2. Add the sugar and milk and bring to the boil. Reduce the heat and simmer for 1 minute.
3. Remove from the heat and strain. Serve hot in a thick glass tumblers.

Index